BIOZONE'S GOING DIGITAL
for iPad and iPod

D1188984

▶ **NEW STUDENT REVIEW SERIES**

Prepare for exams and assignments with these great study aids, adapted from our critically acclaimed Presentation Media.

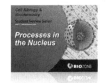

Processes in the Nucleus
- The Molecules of Life
- Introduction to Cells
- Cell Structure
- Cell Membranes & Transport
- Cellular Energetics
- Process in the Nucleus

Non-Infectious Disease
- The Nature of Disease
- Infectious Disease
- Non-infectious Disease
- Defence & the Immune System

Cultural Evolution
- Primate Evolution
- Hominin Evolution
- Cultural Evolution

Practical Ecology
- Introduction to Ecosystems
- Ecological Niche
- Populations & Interactions
- Practical Ecology
- Communities
- Biodiversity & Conservation
- Human Impact

Inheritance
- The Genetic Code
- Mutations
- The Nature of the Gene
- Inheritance
- Gene Interactions

Gene Technology
- Gene Technology

The Origin of Life
- The Origin of life
- The Evidence for Evolution
- The Mechanisms of Evolution
- Patterns of Evolution
- Human Intervention in Evolution

The Lymphatic System & Immunity
- Cells & Tissues
- The Integument & Homeostasis
- Skeletal & Muscular Systems
- The Nervous System
- The Endocrine System
- The Cardiovascular System
- The Lymphatic System & Immunity
- The Respiratory System
- The Digestive System
- The Urinary System
- Reproduction & Development

The Earth's Systems
- The Earth's System
- Ecosystems
- Natural Ecosystem Change
- Populations
- Investigating Ecosystems
- Land & Water
- Energy
- Pollution
- Global Change

PRICE
£1.49 - 2.49*

* Country prices may vary.

PURCHASE VIA THE **FREE BIOZONE** APP

Available on the App Store

EDEXCEL
BIOLOGY 1

A-Level Year 1/AS

MODEL ANSWERS

This model answer booklet is a companion publication to provide answers for the activities in the EDEXCEL Biology 1 Student Workbook. These answers have been produced as a separate publication to keep the cost of the workbook itself to a minimum. All answers to set questions are provided, but chapter reviews are the student's own and no model answer is set. Working and explanatory notes have been provided where clarification of the answer is appropriate.

ISBN 978-1-927309-27-8

Copyright © 2015 Richard Allan
Published by **BIOZONE International Ltd**

Printed by REPLIKA PRESS PVT LTD using paper produced from renewable and waste materials

Additional copies of this Model Answers book may be purchased directly from the publisher.

BIOZONE Learning Media (UK) Ltd.

Telephone local:	01283 530 366
Telephone international:	+44 1283 530 366
Fax local:	01283 831 900
Fax international:	+44 1283 831 900
Email:	sales@biozone.co.uk

www.**BIOZONE**.co.uk

CONTENTS EDEXCEL BIOLOGY 1

Mathematical and Practical Skills in Biology

1   How Do We Do Science? 1
2   Hypotheses and Predictions 1
3   Types of Data 1
4   Making A Qualitative Investigation 1
5   Making A Quantitative Investigation 1
6   Accuracy and Precision 1
7   Working with Numbers 1
8   Fractions, Percentages, and Ratios 1
9   Logs and Exponents 1
10 Properties of Geometric Shapes 2
11 Practising With Data 2
12 Apparatus and Measurement 2
13 Recording Results 2
14 Constructing Tables and Graphs 2
16 Drawing Bar Graphs 3
17 Drawing Histograms 3
18 Drawing Line Graphs 3
19 Correlation or Causation 3
20 Drawing Scatter Plots 4
21 Interpreting Line Graphs 4
23 Spearman Rank Correlation 4
24 Mean, Median, Mode 4
25 Spread of Data 5
26 Interpreting Sample Variability 5
28 Test Your Understanding 5
29 KEY TERMS: Did You Get it? 6

Biological molecules

30 The Biochemical Nature of Cells 6
31 Organic Molecules 6
32 Sugars 6
33 Condensation and Hydrolysis of Sugars 7
34 Colorimetry 7
35 Polysaccharides 7
36 Starch and Cellulose 7
37 Lipids 7
38 Phospholipids 7
39 Amino Acids 8
40 Chromatography 8

41 Protein Shape is Related to Function 8
42 Protein Structure 8
43 Comparing Globular and Fibrous Proteins 8
44 Biochemical Tests 8
45 Nucleotides 8
46 Nucleic Acids 8
47 Determining the Structure of DNA 9
48 Constructing a DNA Model 9
49 DNA Replication 9
50 Enzyme Control of DNA Replication 9
51 Meselson and Stahl's Experiment 9
52 Modelling DNA Replication 10
53 Genes to Proteins 10
54 The Genetic Code 10
55 Cracking the Code 10
56 Transcription in Eukaryotes 10
57 Translation 10
58 Protein Synthesis Summary 10
59 The Nature of Mutations 11
60 Sickle Cell Mutation 11
61 Enzymes 11
62 How Enzymes Work 11
63 Models of Enzyme Activity 11
64 Enzyme Kinetics 11
65 Investigating Catalase Activity 11
66 Enzyme Inhibition 12
67 Inorganic Ions 12
68 Water 12
69 The Properties of Water 12
70 Chapter Review 13
71 KEY TERMS: Did You Get It? 13

Cells, viruses, and reproduction

72 The Cell Theory 13
73 Types of Living Things 13
74 Levels of Organisation 13
75 Cell Sizes 13
76 Prokaryotic Cells 13
77 The Gram Stain and Antibiotic Sensitivity 13
78 Measuring Antibiotic Sensitivity 13
79 Plant Cells 14
80 Identifying Structures in a Plant Cell 14

CONTENTS EDEXCEL BIOLOGY 1

81   Animal Cells 14

82   Identifying Structures in an Animal Cell 14

83   Identifying Organelles 14

84   Cell Structures and Organelles........................ 14

85   Specialisation in Plant Cells 15

86   Specialisation in Human Cells 15

87   Animal Tissues 15

88   Plant Tissues 15

89   Optical Microscopes............................ 16

90   Measuring and Counting Using a Microscope .. 16

91   Calculating Linear Magnification 16

92   Preparing a Slide 16

93   Staining a Slide.................................... 16

94   Practicing Biological Drawings 16

95   Electron Microscopes........................... 16

96   Viruses 16

97   Life Cycle of a Bacteriophage 17

98   Life Cycle of a Retrovirus 17

99   Antiviral Drugs 17

100 Controlling Viral Disease.......................... 17

101 Cell Division 17

102 Mitosis and the Cell Cycle 17

103 Recognising Stages in Mitosis 17

104 Regulation of the Cell Cycle...................... 18

105 Meiosis 18

106 Crossing Over Problems 18

107 Modelling Meiosis 18

108 Mitosis vs Meiosis 18

109 Chromosome Mutations................................ 18

110 Non-Disjunction In Meiosis 18

111 Aneuploidy in Humans.............................. 19

112 Gametes 19

113 Spermatogenesis.................................... 19

114 Oogenesis.. 19

115 Fertilisation and Early Growth.................... 19

116 Reproduction in Plants............................ 20

117 Reproduction in Angiosperms........................ 20

118 Pollination and Fertilisation 20

119 Sucrose Concentration and
     Pollen Tube Growth 20

120 Chapter Review 20

121 KEY TERMS: Did You Get It? 20

Classification and biodiversity

122 Classification Systems.............................. 21

123 How Do We Assign Species? 21

124 The Biological Species Concept 21

125 The Phylogenetic Species Concept................... 21

126 Gel Electrophoresis 21

127 The Principles of DNA Sequencing.................. 21

128   Distinguishing Species by
      Gel Electrophoresis............................. 21

129 Bioinformatics 22

130 Using DNA Probes................................. 22

131 Investigating Genetic Diversity 22

132 Validating New Evidence 22

133 Classification Systems: The Old and the New ... 22

134 Constructing Cladograms 22

135 Mechanism of Natural Selection 23

136 What is Adaptation?................................ 23

137 Adaptation and Niche............................ 23

138 Natural Selection in Pocket Mice................... 24

139 Selection for Skin Colour in Humans 24

140 Isolation and Species Formation.................... 25

141 Reproductive Isolation 25

142 Allopatric Speciation 25

143 Sympatric Speciation 25

144 Stages in Species Development 25

145 Antibiotic Resistance.............................. 26

146 Antigenic Variability in Viruses 26

147 Resistance in HIV 26

148 Chloroquine Resistance in Protozoa 26

149 Biodiversity 26

150 Sampling Populations 26

151 Interpreting Samples............................. 27

152 Assessing Species Diversity 27

153 Investigating Biodiversity........................ 27

154 Assessing Diversity at the Genetic Level 27

155 How Human Activity Affects Biodiversity 27

156 Why is Biodiversity Important?................... 28

157 Hedgerows.. 28

158 *In-Situ* Conservation 28

159 *Ex-situ* Conservation............................ 28

160 Chapter Review.................................... 28

161 KEY TERMS: Did You Get It?...................... 28

CONTENTS EDEXCEL BIOLOGY 1

Exchange and transport

162 The Structure of Membranes 28

163 How Do We Know? Membrane Structure 29

164 Factors Altering Membrane Permeability 29

165 Diffusion 30

166 Osmosis 30

167 Water Movement in Plant Cells 30

168 Making Dilutions 30

169 Estimating Osmolarity....................................... 30

170 Diffusion and Cell SIze 31

171 Active Transport 31

172 Ion Pumps 31

173 Endocytosis and Exocytosis 31

174 Active and Passive Transport Summary 32

175 ATP Supplies Energy for Work 32

176 Introduction to Gas Exchange 32

177 Gas Exchange in Animals................................. 32

178 The Human Gas Exchange System................... 32

179 Breathing in Humans 32

180 Investigating Ventilation Rate in Humans........... 33

181 Gas Exchange in Insects 33

182 Dissection of an Insect..................................... 33

183 Gas Exchange in Fish...................................... 248

184 Gas Exchange in Plants.................................... 33

185 Transport in Multicellular Organisms................. 33

186 Closed Circulatory Systems.............................. 34

187 The Mammalian Transport System 34

188 Arteries.. 34

189 Veins 34

190 Capillaries.. 34

191 Capillary Network 34

192 The Role and Formation of Tissue Fluid.............. 34

193 The Human Heart 35

194 Dissection of a Mammalian Heart 35

195 The Cardiac Cycle 35

196 Control of Heart Activity.................................... 35

197 Recording Changes in Heart Rate 35

198 Review of the Human Heart 35

199 Blood 36

200 Blood Clotting 36

201 Atherosclerosis.. 36

202 CVD Risk Factors 36

203 Reducing the Risk 36

204 Haemoglobin and Myoglobin 37

205 Gas Transport in Humans.................................. 37

206 Plant Systems.. 37

207 Vascular Tissue in Plants.................................. 37

208 Xylem... 37

209 Phloem 37

210 Identifying Xylem and Phloem 38

211 Uptake at the Root.. 38

212 Transpiration 38

213 Investigating Plant Transpiration 38

214 Translocation.. 38

215 Experimental Evidence for Plant Transport........... 39

216 Chapter Review.. 39

217 KEY TERMS: Did You Get It?............................ 39

1. How Do We Do Science? (page 5)
1. Citations support the statements made in the text and show you have researched the topic. Referencing helps identify the sources of the citation for validation and for future checking.

2. Student's own response, but should reflect that science is not a linear process and ideas can change with the acquisition of new knowledge.

2. Hypotheses and Predictions (page 6)
1. (a) There are several hypotheses that could be generated to explain these observations.
   - Bright colour patterns might signal to potential predators that the caterpillars are distasteful.
   - Inconspicuous caterpillars are good to eat and their cryptic colouration reduces the chance that they will be discovered and eaten.
   (b) Null forms of these hypotheses:
   - There is no difference in palatability between the bright and cryptically coloured caterpillars.
   - There is no difference between the cryptic and brightly coloured caterpillars in the ease with which they are detected by predators.
   (c) Possible assumptions:
   - Birds and other predators have colour vision.
   - Birds and other predators can learn about the palatability of their prey by tasting them.
   (d) Prediction 1: That birds will avoid preying on brightly coloured, conspicuous caterpillars.
   Prediction 2: Naive (inexperienced) birds will learn from a distasteful experience with an unpalatable caterpillar species and will avoid them thereafter.
   Prediction 3: Birds will prey readily on cryptically coloured caterpillars if these are provided as food.

3. Types of Data (page 7)
1. (a) Skin colour: ranked data.
   (b) Number of eggs: quantitative data, discontinuous.
   (c) Tree trunk diameter: quantitative data, continuous.

2. Quantitative data are more easily analysed in a meaningful way, e.g. by using descriptive statistics.

3. Examples include: gender, viability (dead or alive), species, presence or absence of a feature, flower colour. These data are categorical; no numerical value can be assigned to them.

4. The students should express the abundance of plant species quantitatively, e.g. as percentage cover of a specific species or the number of individual plants present.

4. Making a Qualitative Investigation (page 8)
1. (a) All samples had to be heated for the same amount of time to ensure they all received the same treatment conditions for reaction.
   (b) Stirring ensures maximum contact of substrate and enzyme therefore maximising reaction.

2. As the bananas ripen, the starch is converted to simple sugars fructose and glucose.

3. (a) Fructose is a ketose sugar, but it is converted to glucose in the basic reagent and the aldehyde group gives a positive test.
   (b) You cannot tell from the test results if the banana ripening resulted in conversion of starch to glucose alone or to fructose (fruit sugar) and glucose.

5. Making a Quantitative Investigation (page 9)
1. Aim: To investigate the effect of temperature on the rate of catalase activity.

2. Hypothesis: The rate of catalase activity is dependent on temperature.

3. (a) Independent variable: Temperature.
   (b) 10-60°C in uneven steps: 10°C, 20°C, 30°C, 60°C.
   (c) Unit: °C

   (d) Equipment: A means to maintain the test-tubes at the set temperatures, e.g. water baths. Equilibrate all reactants to the required temperatures in each case, before adding enzyme to the reaction tubes.

4. (a) Dependent variable: Height of oxygen bubbles.
   (b) Unit: mm
   (c) Equipment: Ruler; place vertically alongside the tube and read off the height (directly facing).

5. (a) Each temperature represents a treatment.
   (b) No. of tubes at each temperature = 2
   (c) Sample size: for each treatment = 2
   (d) Times the investigation repeated = 3

6. Tubes 9 and 10 are the controls.

7. Controlled variables (a-c in any order):

   (a) **Catalase and H_2O_2 from the same batch source and with the same storage history**. Storage and batch history can be determined.
   (b) **Equipment of the same type and size** (i.e. using test-tubes of the same dimensions, as well as volume). This could be checked before starting.
   (c) **Same person doing the measurements of height each time**. This should be decided beforehand.
   Note that some variables were controlled: The test-tube volume, and the volume of each reactant. Control of measurement error is probably the most important after these considerations.

6. Accuracy and Precision (page 11)
1. Accuracy refers to the correctness of the measurement, or how close a measurement is to the true value. Precision refers to the repeatability of the measurements (how close the measured values are to each other).

2. (a) 6   (d) 5
   (b) 2   (e) 6
   (c) 1   (f) 2

7. Working With Numbers (page 12)
1. 5600 mm^3

2. 43 000 i.e. 43 x 1000

3. 15 i.e. 3 x 70 = 210 ÷ 10 = 21.
   210 ÷ 20 = 10.5 and 15 is halfway between 21 and 10.5

4. 33, i.e. 66 ÷ 2

5. 45 000 + 645 000

6. 690 000

7. 6.9×10^5

8. Fractions, Percentages, and Ratios (page 13)
1. (a) 28 : 14 : 3: 2: 1 Divide all values by 5
   (b) Interphase = 2800
       Prophase = 1400
       Telophase = 300
       Metaphase = 200
       Anaphase = 100

2. (a) 1/3   (b) 14/15   (c) 1/11

3. 1/3
   (5/20 x 6 = 30/120) + (5/12 x 10 = 50/120) = 2/3. 2/3 ÷ 2 = 1/3

4. **% lean body mass**
   Athlete: 76.0%
   Lean   73.2%
   Normal weight   70.8%
   Overweight   60.0%
   Obese   54.7%

9. Logs and Exponents (page 14)
1. As body mass increases, basal metabolic rate decreases.

2. In power functions, the base value is variable and the exponent is fixed. In exponential functions the base value is fixed and the exponent is variable.

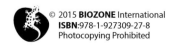

3. (a) A log transformation is used in data that is increasing exponentially.
    (b) Log transformations normalise data and make large numbers easier to work with.

10. Properties of Geometric Shapes (page 15)
1. (a) 12.5 cm (b) 50.2 cm^2 (c) 33.5 cm^3

2. (a) 13 mm^2 (b) 1.8 cm^3

3. (a) 489.5 cm^2 (b) 829.7 cm^3

4. $48 = l \times w \times h$
    $8 = 4 \times 2.5 \times h$
    $h = 48/10 = 4.8$

5. $27 = \pi r^2 h = \pi r^2 \times 3$
    $27/3 = \pi r^2$
    $27/3\pi = r^2$
    $\sqrt{27/3\pi} = r$
    $r = 1.69$

6. (a) SA $= 4\pi r^2 = 4\pi \times 0.2^2 = 0.50$ μm^2
    (b) V $= 4/3 \times \pi r^3 = 4/3 \times \pi \times 0.2^3 = 0.033$ μm^3
    (c) 80% of 0.2 = 0.16. SA $= 4\pi r^2 = 4\pi \times 0.16^2 = 0.32$ μm
    (d) V $= 4/3 \times \pi r^3 = 4/3 \times \pi \times 0.16^3 = 0.017$ μm^3
    (e) Original cell 0.5/0.033 = 15.1 = 15:1
         New cell 0.32/0.017 - 18.8 = 19:1

11. Practising With Data (page 16)
1. Performing data transformations:
    (a) Photosynthetic rate at different light intensities:

Light intensity	Average time (min)	Reciprocal of time (min^{-1})
100	15	0.067
50	25	0.040
25	50	0.020
11	93	0.011
6	187	0.005

    (b) Water loss with bubble potometer

Time	Pipette arm reading (cm^3)	Plant water loss (cm^3 min^{-1})
0	9.0	-
5	8.0	0.2
10	7.2	0.16
15	6.2	0.2
20	4.9	0.26

    (c) Incidence of cyanogenic clover in different regions:

Clover type	Frost free No.	Frost free %	Frost prone No.	Frost prone %	Totals
Cyanogenic	124	78	26	18	150
Acyanogenic	35	22	115	82	150
Total	159	100	141	100	300

    (d) Frequency of size classes of eels:

Size class (mm)	Frequency	Relative frequency (%)
0-50	7	2.6
50-99	23	8.5
100-149	59	21.9
150-199	98	36.3
200-249	50	18.5
250-299	30	11.1
300-349	3	1.1
Total	270	100.0

2. (a) 8.970×10^3 (b) 4.6×10^{-2} (c) 1.467851×10^6
3. (a) 0.43 (b) 0.000031 (c) 62 000
4. (a)

Chilli Beans Nutrition Facts Serving size 1 cup (253 g)		
Amount per serving		% Composition
Total Fat	8 g	3.2
– Saturated Fat	3 g	1.2
Total Carbohydrate	22 g	8.7
– Dietary Fibre	9 g	3.5
– Sugars	4 g	1.6
Protein	25 g	9.9

    (b) Dietary fibre 3.5% Sugars: 1.6%
    (c) 72%

12. Apparatus and Measurement (page 17)
1. (a) 25 mL graduated cylinder
    (b) 50 mL graduated cylinder
    (c) 10 mL pipette

2. (a) $((98-100)/100) \times 100 = -2\%$
    (b) $((9.98-10/10) \times 100 = -0.2\%$
    (c) The greater the sample value the lower the percentage error when the error value remains constant.

13. Recording Results (page 18)
1. See table below.

2. The table would be three times as big in the vertical dimension; the layout of the top of the table would be unchanged. The increased vertical height of the table would accommodate the different ranges of the independent variable (full light, as in question 1, but also half light, and low light). These ranges would have measured values attached to them (they should be quantified, rather than subjective values).

14. Constructing Tables and Graphs (page 19)
1. The two means are not significantly different because the 95% CIs overlap. The mean at 4 gm^{-3} has such a large 95% CI we cannot be confident that it is significantly different from the mean at 3 gm^{-3}.

		Trial 1 [CO$_2$] in ppm (day 0)											Trial 2 [CO$_2$] in ppm (day 2)											Trial 3 [CO$_2$] in ppm (day 4)										
		Minutes											Minutes											Minutes										
	Set up no.	0	1	2	3	4	5	6	7	8	9	10	0	1	2	3	4	5	6	7	8	9	10	0	1	2	3	4	5	6	7	8	9	10
Full light conditions	1																																	
	2																																	
	3																																	
	Mean																																	

© 2015 **BIOZONE** International
ISBN:978-1-927309-27-8
Photocopying Prohibited

2. Graphs and tables provide different ways of presenting information. Tables summarise raw data, provide an accurate record of the data values, and can record summary statistics. Graphs present information in a way that make trends and relationships in the data apparent. Both are valuable.

16. Drawing Bar Graphs (page 21)

1. (a)

Species	Site 1	Site 2
Ornate limpet	21	30
Radiate limpet	6	34
Limpet sp. A	38	-
Limpet sp. B	57	39
Limpet sp. C	-	2
Catseye	6	2
Topshell	2	4
Chiton	1	3

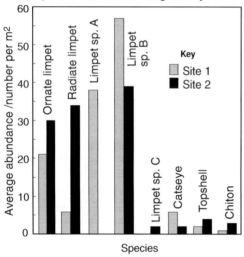

Average abundance of eight mollusc species at two sites along a rocky shore

17. Drawing Histograms (page 22)

1. (a)

Weight / kg	Total
45-49.9	1
50-54.9	2
55-59.9	7
60-64.9	13
65-69.9	15
70-74.9	13
75-79.9	11
80-84.9	16
85-89.9	9
90-94.9	5
95-99.9	2
100-104.9	0
105-109.9	1

(b)

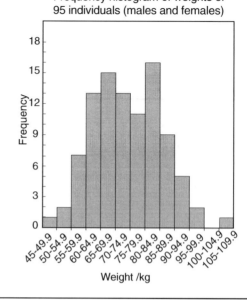

Frequency histogram of weights of 95 individuals (males and females)

18. Drawing Line Graphs (page 23)

1. (a)

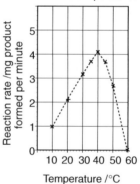

Rate of reaction of enzyme A at different temperatures

(b) Rate of reaction at 15°C = 1.6 mg product min^{-1}

2. (a) Line graph and (b) point at which shags and nests were removed: See graph top of next page.

19. Correlation or Causation (page 25)

1. A correlation between variables does not mean that one variable caused or is even related to the other.

2. (a)

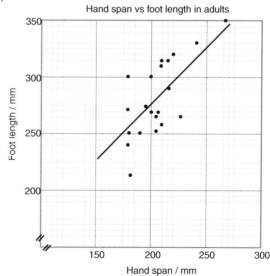

Hand span vs foot length in adults

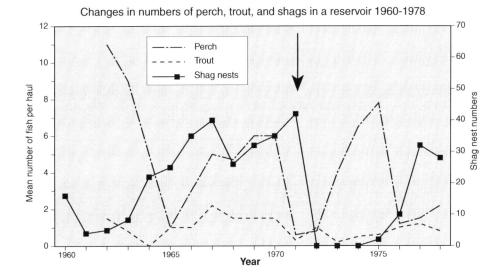

Changes in numbers of perch, trout, and shags in a reservoir 1960-1978

(b) There is a general trend in that a larger hand span will have a longer foot length.

(c) There is a positive relationship between hand span and foot length but it is not very strong. ($r^2 = 0.5$ calc. in Excel)

---

20. Drawing Scatter Plots (page 26)

1. (a) and (b): Scatter plot and fitted curve:

Oxygen consumption of fish with affected gills

2. (a) **At rest**: No clear relationship. The line on the graph appears to have no significant slope and although here is a slight tendency for oxygen consumption to fall as more of the gill becomes affected, the scatter makes this relationship inconclusive.

   (b) **Swimming**: A negative linear relationship; the greater the proportion of affected gill, the lower the oxygen consumption.

3. The gill disease appears to have little or no effect on the oxygen uptake in resting fish.

---

21. Interpreting Line Graphs (page 27)

1. (a) 2 (2:1) (b) -1 (c) 0

2. (a) 2 (b) 14

3. (a) 1 (b) 2
   (c) 5 (d) Positive straight

---

23. Spearman Rank Correlation (page 29)

Missing values completed at the top of the column:

1. There is no correlation between the volume of a male frigatebird's throat pouch and the frequency (pitch) of the drumming sound made.

2. (a) 0.59
   (b) Negative
   (c) Not significant

Bird	Rank (R₁)	Rank (R₂)	Difference (D) (R₁-R₂)	D²
1	2	3	-1	1
2	1	6	-5	25
3	4	12	-8	64
4	5	4	-1	1
5	3	8.5	-3.5	12.25
6	7	10	-3	9
7	6	11	-5	25
8	9	7	2	4
9	8	8.5	-0.5	0.25
10	10.5	1	9.5	90.25
11	10.5	5	5.5	30.25
12	12	2	10	100
	Σ(Sum)	0		362

r_s value = -0.266

3. Class analysis will vary but there is likely a correlation between these both at the individual an class level.

---

24. Mean, Median, and Mode (page 30)

1. The modal value and associated ranked entries indicate that the variable being measured (swimmers' height) has a bimodal distribution; the data are not normally distributed. Therefore the mean and median are not accurate indicators of central tendency.
   Note: the median differs from the mean; also an indication of a skewed (non-normal) distribution.

2. The modal value and associated ranked entries indicate that the variable being measured (sori per frond) has a bimodal distribution i.e. the data are not normally distributed. Therefore the mean and median are not accurate indicators of central tendency. Note also that the median differs from the mean; also an indication of a skewed (non-normal) distribution.

© 2015 **BIOZONE** International
ISBN:978-1-927309-27-8

3.

Ladybird mass (mg)	Tally	Total
6.2	\	1
6.7	I	1
7.7	\\	2
7.8	\	1
8.0	I	1
8.2	I	1
8.4	I	1
8.8	\\\\	4
8.9	\	1
9.8	\	1
10.1	\	1

Median = 8th value when in rank order = 8.4

Mode = 8.8

Mean = 124.7 ÷ 15 = 8.3

Note: To plot a histogram, missing weight classes would have to be included with values of 0.

25. Spread of Data (page 32)

1. The larger standard deviation for the first data set indicates the spread of data around the central measure is significantly larger than in the second set.

2. (a) 139.31 / 40 = 3.483
   (b) 0.647
   (c) 2.836 - 4.13 (3.483 ± 0.647)
   (d) 75% (30 out of 40)
   (e) It is normally distributed around the mean.

26. Interpreting Sample Variability (page 33)

1. (a) 496/689 values within ± 1sd of the mean = 72% (48±7.8, i.e. between 40.2 and 55.8)
   (b) 671//689 values within ± 2 sd of the mean = 97% (48± 15.6, i.e. between 32.4 and 63.6)
   (c) The data are close to being normally distributed about the mean (normal = 67% of values within 1 sd of mean and 95% of values between 2 sd of mean).

2. The mean and the median are very close.

3. N = 30 data set
   (a) **Mean** = 49.23
   (b) **Median** = 49.5
   (c) **Mode** = 38
   (d) **Sample variance** =129.22
   (e) **Standard deviation** = 11.37

4. N = 50 data set
   (a) **Mean** = 61.44
   (b) **Median** = 63
   (c) **Mode** = 64
   (d) **Sample variance** = 14.59
   (e) **Standard deviation** = 3.82

5. Frequency histogram for the N=50 perch data set.

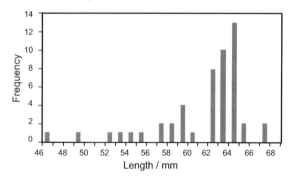

Length / mm

Frequency histogram for the N = 30 perch data set.

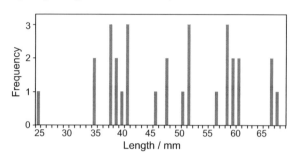

Length / mm

6. (a) The mean and median are very close to each other for the N=30 data set. There is a larger difference between the mean and median values obtained in the N=50 data set.
   (b) The standard deviation obtained for the N=30 set is much larger (11.37) compared to only 3.82 for the larger N=50 data set.
   (c) The N=30 data set more closely resembles the complete data set. The mean and median are quite close to those of the original data set. The mean, median and mode for the N=50 data set are considerably higher than those statistics for the complete data set. The sample variance and standard deviation values for the complete data set fall between those of the two smaller data sets.

7. (a) Histogram for the N=30 data set shows a relatively normal distribution of data. Histogram for the N=50 data set shows a non-normal distribution which is skewed to the right (negative skew).
   (b) The person who collected the sample in the N=30 data set used equipment and techniques designed to collect fish randomly. As a result, a normal distribution of fish sizes was obtained by their sampling methods. Fish collection for the N=50 sample set was biased. The mesh size used did not retain smaller fish, so a larger proportion of bigger fish were collected. When plotted on a frequency histogram the data presented as a negative skew.

28. Test Your Understanding (page 37)

1. Fertiliser concentration.
   Range: 0.0-0.30 g dm^{-3} in steps of 0.06 g dm^{-3}.

2. 5

3. Outlying value = 23.6. This value should not be used in calculations as it is likely it is an anomalous event and could skew the result.

4. Missing values below. For treatment 0.24 g dm^{-3} values are with outlier included (without outlier):

Fertiliser concn	Total mass	Mean mass
0.0	408.5	81.7
0.06	546.3	109.3
0.12	591.4	118.28
0.18	510.1	127.5
0.24	582.5 (558.9)	116.5 (139.7)
0.30	610.4	122.1

© 2015 **BIOZONE** International
ISBN:978-1-927309-27-8
Photocopying Prohibited

5. Completed graph below. Only the plot with outlier excluded is shown.

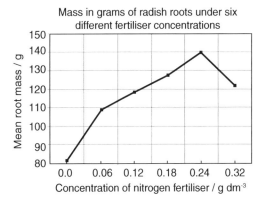

Mass in grams of radish roots under six different fertiliser concentrations

6. The students should have recorded the dry mass of the root, by first drying the root in an oven at low temperature to remove any water.

7. Measuring only the root mass fails to take into account the amount of growth/mass in the leaves.

8. Measuring the mass of the leaves, the number of leaves, the diameter on the root, the length of the root, the length of the leaves etc.

9.

Fertiliser concn	Mean	Median	Mode
0.0	8.6	9	9
0.06	15.6	16	16
0.12	16.6	17	17
0.18	18.2	18	18
0.24	18.5	18.5	No mode
0.30	18.2	18	No mode

10. (a) 6 (0.24 g dm^{-3} sample 1)
    (b) 16
    (c) With outlier 5.02 Without outlier 0.5
    (d) The (biased) mean does not properly reflect the data set when the outlier is included. The standard deviation is vastly increased to accommodate the outlier while all other values are above the (biased) mean and within only one standard deviation.

11. 0.24 g dm^{-3} fertiliser (after removing the outlier).

12. Not all plants in sample may have received the same amount of fertiliser/water. Plants in centre of group may be more shaded/protected.

13. Nitrogen fertiliser increases the growth of radish plants, but only up to a limit, with peak performance reached at 0.24 g dm^{-3} of fertiliser. The fertiliser also increases the number of leaves per plant (up to a limit) which is likely related to the overall increase in growth of the plant.

14. Replication decreases the likelihood of chance events affecting results or may identify true results that may have been attributed to chance. It helps to remove uncontrollable factors and adds weight to the findings.

---

29. KEY TERMS: Did You Get It? (page 40)
1. (a) 6.
   (b) -1
   (c) Negative gradient, variables are inversely proportional.
   (d) y = -5 + 6 = 1

2. (11·71 - 11.75)/11.75 x 100 = -0.34%

---

3. (a) and (b)

Cumulative sweat loss / cm^3	Rate of sweat loss / cm^3 min^{-1}
0	0
50	5
130	8
220	9
560	11.3

(c)

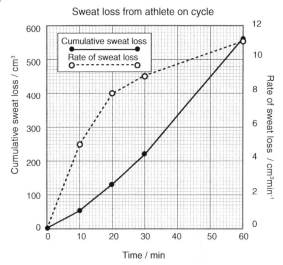

Sweat loss from athlete on cycle

(d) The rate of sweat loss increases but will eventually plateau as the rate of increase reduces.

---

30. The Biochemical Nature of Cells (page 43)
1. A monomer is a repeated component of a larger organic molecule. A polymer is an organic molecule made up a repeated monomers.

2. (a) Carbohydrates: A major structural component of most plant cells, a ready source of energy, and they are involved in cellular recognition. Can be converted to fats.
   (b) Lipids: A ready store of energy (their energy yield per gram is twice that of carbohydrates). They also provide insulation and transport fat-soluble vitamins. Phospholipids are a major component of cellular membranes.
   (c) Proteins: Required for growth and repair of cells and tissues. Roles in catalysing reactions, cell signalling, internal defence, contraction, and transport. Can be converted to fats.
   (d) Nucleic acids, e.g. DNA and RNA, encode the genetic information for the construction and functioning of an organism. Nucleotide derivatives (e.g. ATP) are energy carriers in the cell.

---

31. Organic Molecules (page 31)
1. Carbon, hydrogen, and oxygen.

2. Sulfur and nitrogen.

3. (a) Arrows should indicate the four electrons in the outer shell.
   (b) Four covalent bonds (valency of 4).

4. A molecular (or chemical) formula shows the numbers and kinds of atoms in a molecule whereas a structural formula is the graphical representation of the molecular structure showing how the atoms are arranged.

---

32. Sugars (page 45)
1. (a) Primary energy source for cellular metabolism
   (b) Structural units for disaccharides and polysaccharides (energy sources and structural carbohydrates).

© 2015 **BIOZONE** International
ISBN:978-1-927309-27-8
Photocopying Prohibited

2. Glucose is a hexose sugar (6 carbon atoms) while ribose is a pentose sugar (5 carbon atoms).

3. Isomers have the same molecular formula but their atoms are linked in different sequences. For example, α-glucose and β-glucose are isomers because, although they have the same molecular formula ($C_6H_{12}O_6$), they are structurally different. This difference gives them different chemical properties.

33. Condensation and Hydrolysis of Sugars (page 46)

1. Disaccharide sugars are formed by condensation reactions and broken down by hydrolysis. Condensation reactions join two monosaccharide molecules by a glycosidic bond with the release of a water molecule. Hydrolysis reactions use water to split a disaccharide molecule into two. The water molecule provides a hydrogen atom and a hydroxyl group.

2. A - Condensation, product: maltose
   B - Hydrolysis, products: two glucose molecules

3.

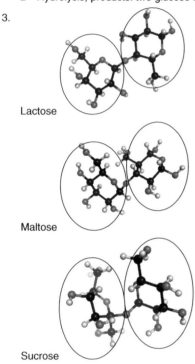

Lactose

Maltose

Sucrose

34. Colorimetry (page 47)

1. (a) Approximately 0.45%
   (b) You would have to dilute the solution so the concentrations fell within the range of the calibration curve.

2. To quantify the glucose concentration of commercial drinks, you would:
   (1) Perform a Benedict's test on each of the commercial drinks.
   (2) Measure and record the absorbance for each sample.
   (3) Determine the glucose concentration of the commercial samples by reading their absorbance off the calibration curve.
   Note: The glucose calibration curve is prepared by measuring the absorbance of a number of known glucose standards.

3. Suspended solids could absorb or refract light, producing an incorrect absorbance for the substance being tested.

35. Polysaccharides (page 48)

1. (a) Polysaccharides are a good source of energy because they are easily hydrolysed into monosaccharides (e.g. glucose) when energy is needed. Monosaccharides are the primary source of cellular fuel.
   (b) Polysaccharides are hydrolysed to produce simpler carbohydrates, e.g. glucose, which can then be transported to other parts of the organism.

2. Glycogen is a highly branched glucose polymer. Its branching makes it compact, more soluble in water than starch, and easily hydrolysed to provide glucose for cellular fuel. Glycogen's properties allow it to be metabolised more quickly, which suits the active lives of moving animals. Starch is a mix of branched and unbranched chains of glucose, which makes it powdery. It is less compact than glycogen, relatively insoluble in cold water, but relatively easy to hydrolyse to soluble sugars, making it a good storage molecule for plants. Cellulose is a linear glucose polymer and is strong and insoluble, which makes it well suited to its role in providing strength and support to plant cells.

36. Starch and Glucose (page 49)

1. (a) Amyloplasts   (b) The cell wall

2. Amylose is a linear molecule formed from glucose molecules held together by α-1, 4 glycosidic bonds. Amylopectin is similar but it also contains α-1, 6 glycosidic bonds, which provide branching points every 20-30 glucose monomers.

3. Cellulose is a linear molecule consisting of several hundred to several thousand β-glucose molecules bonded by a β -1,4 glycosidic bond. Starch is composed of two main molecules; amylose which forms a helix, and a branched molecule, amylopectin.

4. There are more α-1,6 glycosidic bonds in glycogen.

37. Lipids (page 50)

1. (a) Glycerol
   (b) Ester bond
   (c) Fatty acid

2. Fats need more oxidation per gram to form CO_2 than other molecules and so more usable energy can be extracted from the oxidation reactions.

3. (a) Saturated fatty acids contain the maximum number of hydrogen atoms, whereas unsaturated fatty acids contain some double-bonded carbon atoms.
   (b) Saturated fatty acids tend to produce lipids that are solid at room temperature, whereas lipids that contain a high proportion of unsaturated fatty acids tend to be liquid at room temperature.

4. (a) During esterification, a glycerol molecule is joined with a fatty acid. This occurs three times to form a triglyceride.
   (b) Hydrolysis of a triglyceride produces glycerol and three fatty acids

5. Key points for required answer underlined: Lipids are a more concentrated source of energy than carbohydrates or proteins, providing fuel for aerobic respiration through fatty acid oxidation. They are important as energy storage molecules, and carbohydrates and protein can both be converted into fats by enzymes and stored within adipose (fat) cells. Fat absorbs shocks and cushions internal organs such as the kidneys and heart. Stored lipids provide insulation and reduce heat loss to the environment. Lipids are a source of metabolic water, e.g. the camel's hump is a store of fat that can be metabolised to provide water as well as energy. As steroids, they are important as hormones (e.g. aldosterone, testosterone) and transport fat soluble vitamins (e.g. vitamin E). Waxes and oils provide waterproofing to the surfaces of organisms and phospholipids form cellular membranes

38. Phospholipids (page 52)

1. (a) The amphipathic nature of phospholipids (with a polar, hydrophilic end and a hydrophobic, fatty acid end) causes them to orientate in aqueous solutions so that the hydrophobic 'tails' point in together. Hence the bilayer nature of membranes.
   (b) The cellular membranes of an Arctic fish could be expected to contain a higher proportion of unsaturated fatty acids than those of a tropical fish species. This would help them to remain fluid and functional at low temperatures.

2. Unsaturated phospholipids can not pack together as tightly as saturated phospholipids there are more "spaces" within the membrane bilayer, making the membrane more fluid.

39. Amino Acids (page 53)
1. (a) The R group
   (b) The sequence of amino acids in the polypeptide chain.
   (c) The order of nucleotides in DNA and RNA.
   (d) The differences between amino acids are due to the different properties of the R group. These cause different kinds of intermolecular bonding between amino acids in the polypeptide chain, which influences the way the polypeptide will fold up.

2. (a) A peptide bond
   (b) the bond forms by a condensation reaction
   (c)

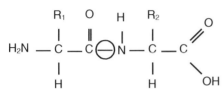

   (d) Di- and polypeptides are broken down by hydrolysis.

40. Chromatography (page 54)
1. Rf = 15 mm ÷ 33 mm = 0.45

2. Rf must always be less than one because the substance cannot move further than the solvent front.

3. Immersion would just wash out the substance into solution instead of separating the components behind a solvent front.

4. (a) A = 0.7 B = 0.5
   (b) A = Alanine   B = Glycine

5. (a) Alanine and arginine
   (b) Their Rf values are very close together.

41. Protein Shape is Related to Function (page 55)
1. The sequence of amino acids (primary structure) determines how a protein folds. The distribution of attractive and repulsive charges on the amino acids determines how the protein is organised and folded (and therefore also determines its biological function).

2. The interior of a plasma membrane is a hydrophobic environment. Channel proteins span the membrane, and fold in such a way that the non-polar (hydrophobic) R-groups align to the outside, and polar (hydrophilic) R-groups form a channel on the inside. This channel allows water soluble molecules to cross the membrane.

3. Denaturation is the process of the protein losing it shape. The loss of shape disrupts the protein's active site and thus its ability to carry out its biological function.

42. Protein Structure (page 56)
1. (a) Peptide bonds between the amino acids.
   (b) α-helices and β-pleated sheets form due to hydrogen bonding.
   (c) Chemical bonds and hydrophobic interactions.
   (d) Interactions between two or more protein molecules or polypeptide chains (subunits).

2. The R groups on each amino acid allow weak intermolecular forces to bind different parts of the polypeptide chain together. This binding causes the polypeptide chain to fold up into the functional shape.

43. Comparing Globular and Fibrous Proteins
(page 57)
1. (a) Proteins form an important component of connective tissues and epidermal structures, cell membranes (regulatory role), and in DNA packing.

   (b) Enzymes are involved in almost all metabolic reactions. Examples include RuBisCo (photosynthesis), lipase (fat digestion), pyruvate dehydrogenase (cellular respiration).

2. Their tertiary structure produces long fibres or sheets, with many cross-linkages. This makes them very tough physically and ideal as structural molecules.

3. Their tertiary structure produces a globular shape with a specific active site that is critical to their interaction with other molecules and their catalytic activity.

44. Biochemical Tests (page 58)
1. Lipids are not soluble in water. Ethanol acts as a non-polar solvent and is able to dissolve lipids, but is also soluble in water. By dissolving the lipids in the alcohol first, they can then form a mixture, or emulsion, with water that will not separate.

2. When the lipid/ethanol solution is added to water, the lipid forms a precipitate and results in a cloudy appearance.

3. The acid hydrolysis splits the non-reducing sugar into its monosaccharides. These can then be analysed with Benedict's solution.

4. They can not be used to determine concentrations or distinguish between different molecules.

45. Nucleotides (page 59)
1. (a) A, T, C, G   (b) A, U, C, G

2. (a) Deoxyribose   (b) Ribose

3. The nucleotides (bases) are stored in a specific sequence that is used by the cellular machinery to code for amino acids that make protein.

46. Nucleic Acids (page 60)
1.

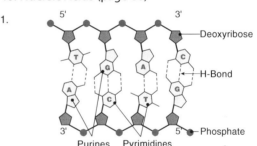

Purines   Pyrimidines

2. (a) The following bases always pair in a normal DS DNA: guanine with cytosine, cytosine with guanine, thymine with adenine, adenine with thymine.
   (b) In mRNA, adenine pairs with uracil (not thymine).
   (c) The hydrogen bonds in double stranded DNA hold the two DNA strands together.

3. mRNAs code for proteins, tRNA moves amino acids to the growing polypeptide chain (to the ribosome binding site), rRNA catalyses formation of a polypeptide.

4. (a) Label uracil or ribose sugar (only found in RNA).
   (b) Label thymine or deoxyribose sugar (only found in DNA).

5. (a) The asymmetric (phosphodiester) bonds in the sugar-phosphate backbone give the molecule a direction so that the two strands in the double-helix run in opposite directions (they are anti-parallel).
   (b) 5' end terminates in a phosphate group, 3' end terminates in a hydroxyl group (from a sugar).

6.

	DNA	RNA
Sugar present	Deoxyribose	Ribose
Bases present	Adenine	Adenine
	Guanine	Guanine
	Cytosine	Cytosine
	Thymine	Uracil
Number of strands	Two (double)	One (single)
Relative length	Long	Short

47. Determining the Structure of DNA (page 62)

1. The gaps labelled A in the diagram made Watson and Crick realise that pattern was produced by a double helix.

2. If a molecule is two stranded with anti-parallel, complementary strands made of bases that follow a strict base pairing rule, then there was a mechanism by which one strand could act as a template for making the other.

3. (a) Protein coding regions are organised into introns (not translated) and exons (translated into proteins).
   (b) Introns may serve regulatory functions in the cell, e.g. as regulatory RNAs including ribosomal RNA (rRNA) and transfer RNAs (tRNA).

48. Constructing a DNA Model (page 63)

3. Labels as follows:

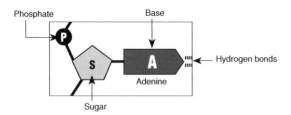

4.and 5. below.

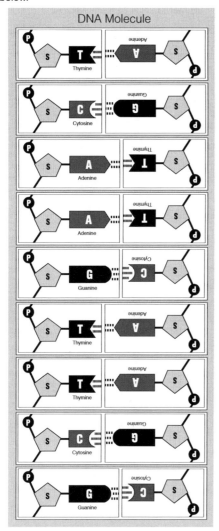

6. Factors preventing mismatch of nucleotides:
   - The number of hydrogen bond attraction points.
   - The size (length) of the base (thymine and cytosine are short, adenine and guanine are long).

Examples: Cytosine will not match cytosine because the bases are too far apart, G will not match G because they are too long to fit side by side; T will not match G and C will not match A because there is a mis-match in the number and orientation of H-bonds.

49. DNA Replication (page 67)

1. DNA replication prepares a chromosome for cell division by producing two chromatids which are identical copies of the genetic information for the chromosome.

2. (a) Step 1: Enzymes unwind DNA molecule to expose the two original strands.
   (b) Step 2: DNA polymerase enzyme uses the two original strands as template to make complementary strands.
   (c) Step 3: The two resulting double-helix molecules coil up to form two chromatids.

3. 44

4. 50% new 50% original

5. It means that each new double strand has one strand that is original (parent) DNA.

6. Nucleotides are added to the 5' end of the new DNA strand, matching bases on the parent DNA with complementary bases on the new DNA strand.

7. The base pairing rule ensures that the correct complementary nucleotides on the new DNA are paired with the bases on the parent stand, producing an identical copy of the original DNA.

8. One strand of DNA can only be copied in short segments because the enzymes can only work in the 5' to 3' direction. DNA must be unzipped a short distance before enzymes can begin copying, and they copy in the opposite direction to which the DNA is unzipped.

9. DNA replication is the process by which the DNA molecule is copied to produce to identical DNA strands. Replication is tightly controlled by enzymes. The enzymes also proofread the DNA during replication to correct any mistakes. DNA replication is required before mitosis can occur. After replication, the chromosome is made up of two chromatids. Each chromatid contains half original and half new DNA. The chromatids separate during mitosis.

50. Enzyme Control of DNA Replication (page 69)

1. Enzymes catalyse the reactions that occur during DNA replication. They unwind the DNA, copy the DNA strands, rejoin DNA sequences, and proofread the DNA to correct mistakes. Enzymes are important in ensuring the same sequence of DNA in the parent cell occurs in the daughter cells so that the cell functions normally.

2. (a) **Helicase**: Unwinds the 'parental' strands.
   (b) **DNA polymerase I**: Hydrolyses the RNA primer and replaces it with DNA.
   (c) **DNA polymerase III**: Elongates the leading strand. It synthesises the new Okazaki fragment until it encounters the primer on the previous fragment.
   (d) **Ligase**: Joins Okazaki fragments into a continuous length of DNA.

3. 16 minutes 40 seconds

4. 6 billion x 2 = 12 billion nucleotides. 12 billion ÷ 100 000 = 120 000 mistakes per cell (many are repaired).

51. Meselson and Stahl's Experiment (page 70)

1. (a) Conservative: The original DNA serves as a complete template with the replicated DNA consisting of two completely DNA new strands.
   (b) Semi-conservative: Each DNA strand acts as a template with each replicated DNA consisting of one original strand and one newly replicated strand.
   (c) Dispersive: The replicated DNA strands have old and new DNA scattered throughout them.

2. *E. coli* were grown in an ^{15}N solution to ensure that the nitrogen atoms in their DNA were all ^{15}N. This allows the DNA

of the first generation to be distinguished from the DNA of subsequent generations once they have been transferred back into a ^{14}N solution.

52. Modelling DNA Replication (page 71)

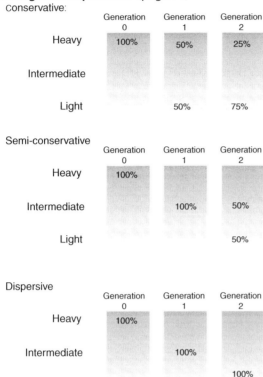

Conservative:

	Generation 0	Generation 1	Generation 2
Heavy	100%	50%	25%
Intermediate			
Light		50%	75%

Semi-conservative

	Generation 0	Generation 1	Generation 2
Heavy	100%		
Intermediate		100%	50%
Light			50%

Dispersive

	Generation 0	Generation 1	Generation 2
Heavy	100%		
Intermediate		100%	
Light			100%

1. (a) Results match the semi-conservative model.
   (b) Yes

2. (a) Conservative
   (b) Dispersive

53. Genes to Proteins (page 74)

1 (a) A triplet   (b) A codon

2 (a) A gene is a section of DNA that codes for a protein. it is the functional unit of heredity.
   (b) RNA polymerase.
   (c) The promoter acts as a region for the RNA polymerase to bind to to start transcription. A terminator indicates where RNA polymerase should stop transcribing.

3. Gene expression is the process of rewriting a gene into a protein. It involves two stages, transcription and translation.

4. Transcription and translation occur only in 5' to 3' direction (polymerases work only 5' to 3' because the OH on the 3' is the active site for forming the phosphodiester bond).

54. The Genetic Code (page 75)

1. This exercise demonstrates the need for a 3-nucleotide sequence for each codon and the resulting degeneracy in the genetic code.

Amino acid	Codons						No.
Alanine	GCU	GCC	GCA	GCG			4
Arginine	CGU	CGC	CGA	CGG	AGA	AGG	6
Asparagine	AAU	AAC					2
Aspartic Acid	GAU	GAC					2
Cysteine	UGU	UGC					2
Glutamine	CAA	CAG					2
Glutamic Acid	GAA	GAG					2
Glycine	GGU	GGC	GGA	GGG			4
Histidine	CAU	CAC					2
Isoleucine	AUU	AUC	AUA				3

Leucine	UAA	UUG	CUU	CUC	CUA	CUG	6
Lysine	AAA	AAG					2
Methionine	AUG						1
Phenylalanine		UUU	UUC				2
Proline	CCU	CCC	CCA	CCG			4
Serine	UCU	UCC	UCA	UCG	AGU	AGC	6
Threonine	ACU	ACC	ACA	ACG			4
Tryptophan	UGG						1
Tyrosine	UAU	UAC					2
Valine	GUU	GUC	GUA	GUG			4

2. (a) 16 amino acids
   (b) Two-base codons (e.g. AT, GG, CG, TC, CA) do not give enough combinations with the 4-base alphabet (A, T, G and C) to code for the 20 amino acids.

3. Many of the codons for a single amino acid vary in the last base only. This would reduce the effect of point mutations, creating new and potentially harmful amino acid sequences in only some instances. **Note**: Only 61 codons are displayed above. The remaining three are **terminator** (STOP) codons. These are considered the 'punctuation' or controlling codons that mark the end of a gene sequence. The amino acid **methionine** (AUG) is regarded as the 'start' (initiator) codon.

55. Cracking the Genetic Code (page 76)

1. (a) 4
   (b) 20
   (c) A one or two base code would not produce enough amino acids (4 and 16 amino acids respectively).

2. Only 20 amino acids are produced because some amino acids are encoded by more than one codon.

3. (a) To destroy bacterial DNA so no mRNA could be made.
   (b) If no DNase was added, mRNA could have been copied from the DNA. This would mean there would have been a combination of bacterial mRNA and synthetic mRNA in the extract. That would make it impossible to tell what the amino acids produced from the synthetic extract were.

56. Transcription in Eukaryotes (page 77)

1. mRNA carries a copy of the genetic instructions from the DNA (master instructions) to ribosomes in the cytoplasm. The rate of protein synthesis can be increased by making many copies of identical mRNA from the same piece of DNA.

2. (a) AUG   (b) UAA, UAG, UGA

3. (a) AUG AUC GGC GCU AAA
   (b) AUG UUC GGA UAU UUU

57. Translation (page 78)

1. AUG AUC GGC GCU AAA

2. (a) 61
   (b) There are 64 possible codons for mRNA, but three are terminator codons. 61 codons for mRNA require 61 tRNAs each with a complementary codon.

58. Protein Synthesis Summary (page 79)

1. (a) 1: Unwinding the DNA molecule.
   (b) 2: mRNA synthesis: Nucleotides added to the growing strand of messenger RNA molecule.
   (c) 3: DNA rewinds into double helix structure.
   (d) 4: mRNA moves through nuclear pore in nuclear membrane to the cytoplasm.
   (e) 5: tRNA molecule brings in the correct amino acid to the ribosome.
   (f) 6: Anti-codon on the bottom of the tRNA matches with the correct codon on the mRNA and drops off the amino acid.
   (g) 7: tRNA leaves the ribosome.
   (h) 8: tRNA molecule is recharged with another amino acid, ready to participate in protein synthesis.

2. (a) DNA   (f) Nuclear pore
   (b) Free nucleotides   (g) tRNA

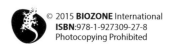

© 2015 **BIOZONE** International
ISBN:978-1-927309-27-8
Photocopying Prohibited

(c) RNA polymerase enzyme (h) Amino acids
(d) mRNA   (i) Ribosome
(e) Nuclear membrane   (j) Polypeptide chain

3. (a) Whether or not the protein is required by the cell
         (regulated by control of gene expression).
    (b) Whether or not there is an adequate pool of the amino
         acids and tRNAs required for the particular protein in
         question.

59. The Nature of Mutations (page 80)

1. A **frame shift mutation** occurs when the sequence of bases
    is offset by one position (by adding or deleting a base). This
    alters the order in which the bases are grouped as triplets and
    can severely alter the amino acid sequence.

2. (a) Reading frame shifts and nonsense substitutions.
    (b) They may cause large scale disruption of the coded
         instructions for making a protein. Either a completely
         wrong amino acid sequence for part of the protein or a
         protein that is partly completed (missing amino acids due
         to an out-of-place terminator codon).
    (c) A substitution mutation to the third base in a codon.
         Because of degeneracy in the genetic code, a substitution
         at the third base position may not change the amino acid
         that is encoded.

3. (a) Mutated DNA: AAA ATA TTT CTC CAA GAT
         mRNA: UUU UAU AAA GAG GUU CUA
         Amino acids: Phe Tyr Lys Glu Val Leu
    (b) ATG → UAC →Tyr = Tyrosine
    (c) No effect because of code degeneracy; both UAC and
         UAU code for Tyr.

60. Sickle Cell Mutation (page 81)

1. (a) Bases: 21   (b) Triplets: 7   (c) Amino acids: 7

2. (a) A point mutation, a base substitution, causes one amino
         acid to change in the β- chain of the haemoglobin
         molecule.
    (b) The mutated haemoglobin protein behaves differently
         to the normal haemoglobin, so that when not carrying
         oxygen, it precipitates out into fibres which deform the
         RBC to a sickle cell shape.
    (c) Heterozygotes (carriers) of the sickle cell mutation have
         both normal and mutated haemoglobin molecules. The
         have enough functional haemoglobin to carry sufficient
         oxygen, so only suffer minor effects of the disease.
    (d) The mutated haemoglobin is less soluble at low oxygen
         tensions. In low oxygen environments (such as at altitude)
         the mutated haemoglobin will precipitate out and the
         carrier will show symptoms of sickle cell disease.

3. The sickle cell mutation affords some degree of resistance to
    malaria and so persists where malaria is present.

61. Enzymes (page 82)

1. (a) The active site is the region where substrate is drawn in
         and positioned in such a way as to promote the reaction.
         The properties of the active site are a function of the
         precise configuration of the amino acid side chains which
         interact with the substrate.
    (b) The active site is very specific because of how the protein
         folds up (its tertiary structure). It will normally accept only
         one type of molecule (the substrate, which has the correct
         configuration to interact with the active site).

2. Substrate molecules must collide with the active site.

3. (a) Large molecules are often too big to enter the cell and
         must be broken down to smaller molecules.
    (b) Extracellular enzymes, such as trypsin, could damage
         internal proteins if produced in an active form.

62. Models of Enzyme Activity (page 83)

1. The lock and key model proposed that the substrate was
    simply drawn into a closely matching cleft (active site) on
the enzyme. In this model, the enzyme's active site was a
somewhat passive recipient of the substrate. Subsequent
studies of enzyme inhibitors showed this assumption to be
incorrect and the model required modification.

2. The induced fit model is a modified version of the lock and key
    in which the substrate and the active site interact. Substrate
    binding causes the active site to change slightly so that bonds
    in the substrate(s) are destabilised. This model is supported
    by evidence from studies of enzyme inhibition.

63. How Enzymes Work (page 84)

1. Enzymes are biological molecules (usually proteins) that
    act as catalysts, allowing reactions to proceed more readily.
    They do this by influencing bond stability in the reactants
    and thereby lowering the activation energy required to create
    an unstable transition state in the substrate from which the
    reaction proceeds readily.

2. A catabolic reaction breaks down complex molecules and use
    energy. Anabolic reactions build complex molecules using
    energy.

64. Enzyme Kinetics (page 85)

1. $(2.4 - 1.4) \div 130 - 72 = 0.017\ cm^3s^{-1}$

2. (a) Approximate numbers given. $(3.5 - 2.5) \div (125 - 50) =$
         $0.013\ cm^3s^{-1}$
    (b) $(2.5 - 1) \div (50 - 10) = 0.0375\ cm^3s^{-1}$

3. (a) Reactants would need to be constantly added to the mix.
    (b) The reactants are being used up.

4. (a) If the substrate is not limited, the reaction rate will
         increase as the concentration of enzyme is increased.
    (b) A cell may increase the rate of protein synthesis
         (transcription and translation) to increase the amount of
         enzyme present, or inactivate enzymes (e.g. by feedback
         inhibition) to reduce their activity.

5. The rate changes (levels off) because, after a certain
    concentration of substrate, the enzymes are saturated by the
    substrate and the reaction rate cannot increase.

6. (a) An optimum temperature for an enzyme is the
         temperature where enzyme activity is maximal.
    (b) Most enzymes perform poorly at low temperatures
         because chemical reactions occur slowly or not at all at
         low temperatures (enzyme activity will reappear when the
         temperature increases; usually enzymes are not damaged
         by low temperatures).
    (c) Reaction rate at $T°C = 2.4 \div 30 = 0.08\ cm^3s^{-1}$
         Reaction rate at $T + 10°C = 4 \div 27 = 0.15\ cm^3s^{-1}$
         $Q_{10} = 1.88$

7. (a) Optimum pH: pepsin: 1-2, trypsin: approx. 7.5-8.2, urease:
         approx. 6.5-7.0.
    (b) The stomach is an acidic environment which is the ideal
         pH for pepsin, whereas trypsin works in the alkaline
         environment of the small intestine. The optimal pH of
         urease suits a neutral environment (it is found in soil and
         bacteria and fungi).

65. Investigating Catalase Activity (page 87)

1. $2H_2O_2 \rightarrow 2H_2O + O_2$

2. (a)-(c), mean, standard deviation, and mean rate below.

Stage	Mean	Std Dev	Mean rate ($cm^3\ s^{-1}\ g^{-1}$)
0.5	10.1	0.5	0.03
2	34.9	3.8	0.12
4	65.5	5.0	0.22
6	36.7	4.0	0.12
10	22.5	2.7	0.08

3. (a) The values obtained for the 0.5 days and 10 days of
         germination are not in accordance with those obtained by

the other groups (trials). The other values are of a similar magnitude.

(b) If the new data are used, the mean should exclude those two values and be calculated using only 5 (rather than 6) trials for those germination stages.

(c) These data values are clearly well adrift from the other values obtained for those stages from other groups (trial); if plotted as a scatter plot, they are distinct outliers on the plot. This suggests that something was wrong with either the measurement or the execution of the trial. It is reasonable therefore to exclude them from the analysis.

4.

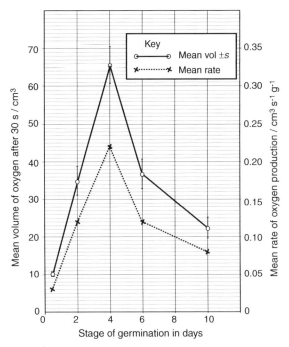

Catalase activity in relation to stage of germination in mung bean seedlings

Key
o——o Mean vol $\pm s$
x······x Mean rate

X-axis: Stage of germination in days
Left Y-axis: Mean volume of oxygen after 30 s / cm^3
Right Y-axis: Mean rate of oxygen production / $cm^3 \ s^{-1} \ g^{-1}$

5. (a) The volume and rate of oxygen production increases rapidly to a peak at 4 days and declines, almost as sharply between 4 and 10 days.

(b) Catalase activity in the sprouting seeds increases rapidly in the first 4 days of germination linked to the increase in cell activity and high respiration rates in early growth. It then falls off as the seedlings become established and metabolism slows.

(c) In part but the fall off in activity was not predicted.

6. Errors include: The equipment could leak around the bung or the tubing. There could be a delay in delivering all the H_2O_2 so a slight delay in correctly timing the start of the reaction. The seeds might not be completely crushed, or crushed to different degrees so that not all the catalase is released.

7. Validity of data could be affected by (two of): insufficient usable data, highly variable data (overlapping data between times), old or poorly stored beans, old or poorly stored H_2O_2, precise, reliable but inaccurate data because of gas losses through the equipment.

66. Enzyme Inhibition (page 89)

1. In **competitive inhibition**, the inhibitor competes with the substrate for the enzyme's active site and, once in place, prevents substrate binding. A **noncompetitive inhibitor** does not occupy the active site but binds to some other part of the enzyme, making it less able to perform its function as an effective biological catalyst.

2. (a) With a competitive inhibitor present, the effect of the competition can be overcome by increasing the substrate concentration; the rate of the reaction will slow, but will eventually reach the same level as that achieved without

an inhibitor. In a system where there is a non-competitive inhibitor, the rate of the reaction slows and is well below the maximum that can be achieved without an inhibitor. This rate depression cannot be overcome by increasing the substrate concentration.

(b) Type of inhibition could be tested by increasing the substrate concentration. If this overcame the rate depression then the inhibition is competitive.

3. Allosteric regulators attach to a site on the enzyme other than the active site and can inhibit enzyme activity. Removal of the regulator reactivates the enzyme. By increasing or decreasing the number of allosteric regulators, a cell can increase or decrease enzyme activity.

4. Many metabolic pathways can be controlled by negative feedback when the end product of a pathway is an inhibitor of an enzyme in the pathway. For example, pyruvate dehydrogenase is inhibited by NADH, a product of the respiration pathway that pyruvate dehydrogenase is part of.

67. Inorganic Ions (page 91)

1. (a) A cation ion is a positively charged ion.
    (b) An anion is a negatively charged ion.

2. Calcium is involved in cell signalling and, as a component of calcium pectate, it helps bind the cell walls of adjacent cells together, providing structural stability.

3. NO_3^- is the source of nitrogen for plants and is important in the formation of amino acids and nucleotides.

4. (a) Some amino acids, some proteins, and coenzyme A.
    (b) Sulfate.
    (c) Animals get their sulfur from eating the protein components of plant and animal tissues.

5. Phosphate is important for the production of ATP and it is a component of phospholipids (cellular membranes) and nucleotides (nucleic acids).

6. The plant would begin to lose its green colour as less chlorophyll would be made.

68. Water (page 92)

1. δ symbol omitted for clarity

Water surrounding a positive ion (Na^+)

Water surrounding a negative ion (Cl^-)

2. Hydrogen bonds form between hydrogen and a strongly electronegative element such as oxygen. In water, hydrogen bonding helps to hold the water molecules together, making it a stable substance. A relatively large amount of energy is needed to overcome these bonds and separate the water molecules (boiling). A similar bonding occurs between water and other molecules, which makes water a very good solvent.

3. The dipole nature of water allows it form a large number of hydrogen bonds making it a good solvent for many substances, e.g. ionic solids and other polar molecules such as sugars and amino acids. It is therefore readily involved in biochemical reactions.

69. The Properties of Water (page 93)

1. (a) A hydrophobic molecule is not attracted to water whereas a hydrophilic molecule is attracted to water.

(b) Hydrophilic molecules attract water. Hydrogen or ionic-dipole bonds keep the hydrophilic molecule or ion surrounded by water molecules and keep it dissolved. It thus travels through the blood as a dissolved molecule or ion, e.g. Na^+ or glucose. Hydrophobic molecules will not form intermolecular bonds with water and thus will not

© 2015 **BIOZONE** International
ISBN:978-1-927309-27-8
Photocopying Prohibited

dissolve. They must be transported around the body by other methods, often attaching to transport molecules in cells, such as oxygen binding to haemoglobin in the blood.

2. Water absorbs heat energy from the body. The energy breaks the hydrogen bonds between the water molecules and they evaporate. Thus the body feels cooler as heat is transferred from the body to the water in the sweat.

70. Chapter Review (page 94)
No model answer. Summary is the student's own.

71. KEY TERMS: Did You Get it? (page 96)
1. (a)

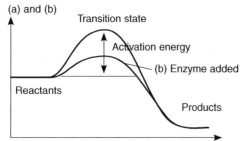

Hydrophilic end (water is attracted to this end)

Hydrophobic end

(b) Hydrophilic head orientates towards water and hydrophobic tail orientates away producing a bilayer with tails innermost.

2. (a) Condensation (b) Hydrolysis

3. (a) Carbohydrates
   (b) Nitrogen
   (c) Sulfur produces disulfide bridges and assists in the folding of the protein and maintaining it structure.

4. mRNA: CUU, UGG, GAA, UGU, AUA, GCA, CGA
   Amino acids: Leu, Trp, Glu, Cys, Lie, Iie, Arg

5. In eukaryotes, gene expression begins with **transcription**, which occurs in the **nucleus**. **Transcription** is the copying of the DNA code into **mRNA**. The **mRNA** is then transported to the **cytoplasm** where **translation** occurs. Ribosomes attach to the **mRNA** and help match the codons on **mRNA** with the anticodons on **tRNA**. The **tRNA** transports the animo acids to the ribosome where they are added to the growing **polypeptide** chain.

6. (a) and (b)

Transition state

Activation energy

(b) Enzyme added

Reactants

Products

7. lipids (D), globular proteins (E), DNA (A), polysaccharides (B), nucleic acids (C)

72. Cell Theory (page 99)
1. Cells are the smallest units of any living thing that display the all the functions of life. Below this level no particular part shows all the functions of life.

2. Organisms such as a *Caulerpa* show multicellular characteristics while being one large cell. Cells do not divide into new cells in the conventional sense.

73. Types of Living Things (page 100)
1. Characteristic features of prokaryotic cells include lack of a membrane-bound nucleus or membrane-bound organelles, typically small cells (0.5-10 μm) with relatively simple organisational structure and a circular chromosome.

2. Characteristic features of eukaryotic cells include the presence of a membrane-bound nucleus and membrane-bound organelles. Large cells with complex cell organisation. DNA is arranged in linear chromosomes.

3. Viruses are classed as non-living because they have

no metabolic machinery of their own. The virus can only metabolise and reproduce by utilising the cellular machinery of a cell it has infected.

74. Levels of Organisation (page 101)
1. (a) The cellular level.
   (b) The organism.
   (c) The chemical level (DNA).

75. Cell Sizes (page 102)
1. (a) *Daphnia*: 1800 μm — 1.8 mm
   (b) *Giardia*: 15 μm — 0.015 mm
   (c) Nucleus 10 μm — 0.01 mm
   (d) *Elodea*: 47 μm — 0.047 mm
   (e) Chloroplast 7 μm — 0.007 mm
   (f) *Paramecium*: 250 μm — 0.25 mm

2. (a) Chloroplast < nucleus < *Giardia* < *Elodea* < *Paramecium* < *Daphnia*
   (b) Visible to naked eye: *Daphnia*

3. (a) 0.00025 mm
   (b) 0.45 mm
   (c) 0.0002 mm

76. Prokaryotic Cells (page 103)
1. (a) The nuclear material (DNA) is not contained within a defined nucleus with a nuclear membrane.
   (b) Membrane-bound cellular organelles (e.g. mitochondria, endoplasmic reticulum) are missing.
   (c) Single, circular chromosome sometimes with accessory chromosomes called plasmids.

2. (a) Locomotion - flagella enable bacterial movement.
   (b) Fimbriae are shorter, straighter, and thinner than flagella. They are used for attachment, not locomotion.

3. The bacterial cell wall lies outside the plasma membrane. It is a semi-rigid structure composed of peptidoglycan, and varying amounts of lipopolysaccharides and lipoproteins.

4. Binary fission is used for cell division (asexual reproduction).

77. The Gram Stain and Antibiotic Sensitivity (page 104)
1. The Gram-stain is used to distinguish between two broad categories of bacteria - Gram-positive and the Gram-negative.

2. The cell walls of Gram-positive bacteria is simple and consists predominantly of many layers of peptidoglycan. The cell walls of Gram-negative bacteria have only a thin innermost layer of peptidoglycan, which is covered by a complex outer lipopolysaccharide layer.

3. The thick, simple peptidoglycan cell walls of Gram-positive bacteria retain the crystal violet stain to give a positive test. The cell walls of Gram-negative bacteria do not retain the crystal violet stain, which is washed out. They are then counterstained with safranin in order to be distinguished.

4. Penicillin inhibits the enzyme that makes the linkages between the peptidoglycan layers of Gram-positive bacterial cell walls. Gram-negative bacteria have much less peptidoglycan and it is located beneath the lipopolysaccharide layer, which cannot be penetrated by the penicillin. Penicillin is therefore largely ineffective against Gram-negative bacteria.

5. The differences in cell wall structure and therefore Gram stain response also relate to the antibiotics that will be effective against the bacteria. It is therefore an important diagnostic test because it will help determine which broad groups of antibiotic will be effective (e.g. antibiotics in the penicillin family will not be effective against gram negative bacteria).

78. Measuring Antibiotic Sensitivity (page 106)
1. (a) A
   (b) 3
   (c) This concentration in most effective as it produces the best result with the least amount of antibiotic used.

© 2015 **BIOZONE** International
ISBN:978-1-927309-27-8
Photocopying Prohibited

79. Plant Cells (page 107)

1. The cell wall provides rigidity, shape, and support for the cell and (through cell turgor) the plant tissues. It also limits the volume of the cell.

2. (a) The vacuole.
   (b) Roles include storage, waste disposal, and growth.

3. (a) Ribosomes in the cytoplasm are 80S ribosomes. Ribosomes in mitochondria and chloroplasts are 70S.
   (b) They have different origins from the cell. 70S ribosomes are also found in bacteria suggesting these organelles have a bacterial origin.

4. Chloroplasts, cell wall

80. Identifying Structures in a Plant Cell (page 108)

1. (a) Cytoplasm
   (b) Vacuole
   (c) Starch granule
   (d) Chloroplast
   (e) Mitochondrion
   (f) Cell wall
   (g) Nucleus
   (h) Chromosome
   (i) Nuclear membrane
   (j) Endoplasmic reticulum
   (k) Plasma membrane

2. 9 cells (1 complete cell, plus the edges of 8 others).

3. Plant cell; it has chloroplasts and a cell wall. It also has a highly geometric cell shape.

4. (a) The cytoplasm is located between the plasma membrane and the nuclear membrane (the material outside the nucleus).
   (b) The cytoplasm comprises a 'watery soup' of dissolved substances. In eukaryotic cells, organelles are found in the cytoplasm.

5. (a) Starch granules, which occur within specialised plastids called leucoplasts. Starch granules are inert inclusions, deposited as a reserve energy store.
   (b) Vacuoles, which are fluid filled cavities bounded by a single membrane. Plant vacuoles contain cell sap, which is an aqueous solution of dissolved food material, ions, waste products, and pigments.

81. Animal Cells (page 109)

1. A: Nucleus   B: Plasma membrane C: Nucleus

2. (a)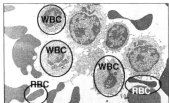
   White blood cells (WBC) & red blood cells (RBC)

   (b) Any of: The RBCs have no nucleus and they are smaller than the white blood cells. The white blood cells have extensions of the plasma membrane (associated with being mobile and phagocytic), are larger than the RBCs, and have a nucleus.

3. – Centrioles (absent from higher plants). They are microtubular structures responsible for forming the poles and the spindles during cell division.
   – Desmosomes. These are points of contact between the plasma membranes of neighbouring cells, which allow cells to combine together to form tissues.

82. Identifying Structures in an Animal Cell (page 110)

1. (a) Plasma membrane
   (b) Golgi apparatus
   (c) Centriole (TS)
   (d) Mitochondrion
   (e) Lysosome
   (f) Nucleus
   (g) Rough ER
   (h) Cytoplasm

2. Centrioles.

3. Plant cells are enclosed by a rigid cellulose cell wall and do not have the capacity for motility or phagocytosis in the way that animal cells do.

4. (a) High protein production and secretion indicated by a relatively large amount of ER and an extensive Golgi.
   (b) Large number of mitochondria indicate that it is metabolically very active (high respiration rate).

5. It has a membrane-bound nucleus and membrane-bound organelles.

83. Identifying Organelles (page 111)

1. (a) Chloroplast
   (b) Plant cells, particularly in leaf and green stems.
   (c) Function: Site of photosynthesis. Captures solar energy to make glucose from CO_2 and water.

2. (a) Golgi apparatus
   (b) Eukaryotic cells (e.g. plant and animal cells)
   (c) Function: Packages substances to be secreted by the cell. Forms a membrane vesicle containing the chemicals for export from the cell (e.g. nerve cells export neurotransmitters, endocrine glands export hormones, digestive gland cells export enzymes).

3. (a) Mitochondrion
   (b) Eukaryotic cells (e.g. plant and animal cells)
   (c) Function: Site of cellular respiration, which releases energy from food (glucose) to fuel metabolism.

(d)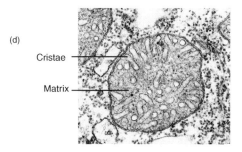
   Cristae
   Matrix

4. (a) Endoplasmic reticulum
   (b) Eukaryotic cells (e.g. plant and animal cells)
   (c) Function: Site of protein and membrane synthesis.
   (d) Ribosomes

5. (a) Nucleus
   (b) Eukaryotic cells (e.g. plant and animal cells)
   (c) Function: Controls cell metabolism and functioning of the whole organism. These instructions are inherited from one generation to the next.

(d)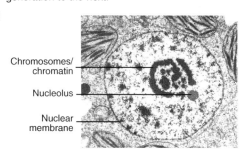
   Chromosomes/ chromatin
   Nucleolus
   Nuclear membrane

84. Cell Structures and Organelles (page 112)

(b) **Name**: Ribosome
   Location: In cytoplasm.
   Function: Protein synthesis (reading mRNA and catalyse addition of amino acids to polypeptide chain.
   Visible with light microscope: No

(c) **Name**: Smooth and rough endoplasmic reticulum
   Location: Penetrates the whole cytoplasm
   SER function: Site of lipid and carbohydrate metabolism.
   RER function: Synthesis of proteins for secretion.
   Visible with light microscope: Yes

(d) **Name**: Vacuole
   Location: Various locations around the cell but often near the centre, especially in plant cells.
   Function: Isolating materials, containing water, providing

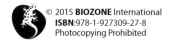
© 2015 **BIOZONE** International
ISBN:978-1-927309-27-8
Photocopying Prohibited

support, maintaining internal cell pressure, maintaining pH.
Visible with light microscope: yes
(e) **Name**: Golgi apparatus
Location: In cytoplasm associated with the smooth endoplasmic reticulum, often close to the nucleus.
Function: Final modification of proteins and lipids. Sorting and storage for use in the cell or packaging molecules for export.
Visible with light microscope: Yes
(f) **Name**: Cellulose cell wall
Location: Surrounds the cell and lies outside the plasma membrane.
Function: Provides rigidity and strength, and supports the cell against changes in turgor.
Visible with light microscope: Yes
(g) **Name**: Nucleus
Location: Discrete organelle, position is variable.
Function: The control centre of the cell; the site of the nuclear material (DNA).
Visible with light microscope: Yes
(h) **Name**: Chloroplast
Location: Within the cytoplasm
Function: The site of photosynthesis
Visible with light microscope: Yes
(i) **Name**: Mitochondrion
Location: In cytoplasm.
Function: Site of cellular respiration (ATP formation)
Visible with light microscope: Yes

85. Specialisation in Human Cells (page 114)
1. (a) **Phagocytic white blood cell**:
   Features: Phagocytic and highly mobile.
   Role: Destroys pathogens and cellular debris.
 (b) **Erythrocyte**:
   Features: Biconcave cell, lacking mitochondria, nucleus, and most internal membranes. Contains the oxygen-transporting pigment, haemoglobin.
   Role: Uptake, transport, and release of oxygen to the tissues. Some transport of CO_2.
 (c) **Squamous epithelial cell**:
   Features: Thin flat cells that line body surfaces.
   Role: Line body surfaces (including internal spaces), providing a membrane in contact with the extracellular environment on one side and anchored to the body cells on the other.
 (d) **Skeletal muscle cell**:
   Features: Cylindrical shape with banded myofibrils. Capable of contraction (shortening).
   Role: Move voluntary muscles acting on skeleton.
 (e) **Ciliated epitheial cell**:
   Features: Simple cells often with a column shaped appearance. Upper surface of cell contains many cilia.
   Role: Cilia sweep back and forth to move particles or fluid. In the bronchioles of the lungs, cilia sweep dust particles up towards the throat.
 (f) **Motor neurone**:
   Features: Cell body with a long extension (the axon) ending in synaptic bodies. Axon is insulated with a sheath of fatty material (myelin).
   Role: Rapid conduction of motor nerve impulses from the spinal cord to effectors (e.g. muscle).
 (g) **Sperm cell**:
   Features: Motile, flagellated cell with mitochondria. Nucleus forms a large proportion of the cell.
   Role: Male gamete for sexual reproduction. Mitochondria provide the energy for motility.
 (h) **Osteocyte**:
   Features: Cell with calcium matrix around it. Fingerlike extensions enable the cell to be supplied with nutrients and wastes to be removed.
   Role: In early stages, secretes the matrix that will be the structural component of bone. Provides strength.

86. Specialisation in Plant Cells (page 115)
1. (b) **Pollen grain**:
   Features: Small, lightweight, often with spikes.
   Role: houses male gamete for sexual reproduction.
 (c) **Palisade parenchyma cell**:
   Features: Column-shaped cell with chloroplasts.
   Role: Primary photosynthetic cells of the leaf.
 (d) **Epidermal cell**:
   Features: Waxy surface on a flat-shaped cell.
   Role: Provides a barrier to water loss on leaf.
 (e) **Vessel element**:
   Features: Rigid remains of a dead cell. No cytoplasm. End walls perforated. Walls are strengthened with lignin fibres.
   Role: Rapid conduction of water through the stem. Provides support for stem/trunk.
 (f) **Stone cell**:
   Features: Very thick lignified cell wall inside the primary cell wall. The cytoplasm is restricted to a small central region of the cell.
   Role: Protection of the seed inside the fruit.
 (g) **Sieve tube member**:
   Features: Long, tube-shaped cell without a nucleus. Cytoplasm continuous with other sieve cells above and below it. Cytoplasmic streaming is evident.
   Role: Responsible for translocation of sugars etc.
 (h) **Root hair cell**:
   Features: Thin cuticle with no waxy layer. High surface area relative to volume.
   Role: Facilitates the uptake of water and ions

87. Animal Tissues (page 116)
1. The organisation of cells into specialised tissues allows the tissues to perform particular functions. This improves efficiency of function because different tasks can be shared amongst specialised cells. Energy is saved in not maintaining non-essential organelles in cells that do not require them.

2. (a) **Epithelial tissue**: Lining/protection. Lines internal and external body surfaces and protects the structures underneath.
 (b) **Nervous tissue**: Transmits information (via nerve impulses).
 (c) **Muscle tissue**: Creates movement through contraction.
 (d) **Connective tissues**: Binding, support, and protection.

3. (a) Muscle tissue is made up of long muscle fibre cells made up of myofibrils. The myofibrils are made up of contractile proteins actin and myosin, which cause the muscle fibres to contact when stimulated. The contraction results in movement of the organism itself (locomotion) or movement of an internal organ.
 (b) Nervous tissue is made up of neurones which transmit nerve impulses and glial cells which provide support to the neurones. Neurones have several protrusions (dendrites or axons) from their cell body which allow conduction of nerves impulses to target cells.

88. Plant Tissues (page 117)
1. The three plant tissue systems are dermal, vascular, and ground tissue systems.

2. **Collenchyma**
Cell type(s): collenchyma cells
Role: provides flexible support.

   Sclerenchyma
   Cell type(s): sclerenchyma cells
   Role: provides rigid, hard support.

   Root Endodermis
   Cell type(s): endodermal cells
   Role: Selective barrier regulating the passage of substances from the soil to the vascular tissue.

   Pericycle
   Cell type(s): parenchyma cells
   Role: Production of branch roots, synthesis and transport of alkaloids.

   Leaf mesophyll
   Cell type(s): spongy mesophyll, palisade mesophyll

Role: Main site of photosynthesis in the plant.

Xylem
Cell type(s): tracheids, vessels, fibres, parenchyma cells
Role: Conducts water and dissolved minerals in vascular plants.

Phloem
Cell type(s): sieve-tube members, companion cells, parenchyma, fibres, sclereids
Role: transport of dissolved organic material (including sugars) within vascular plants.

Epidermis
Cell type(s): epidermal cells, guard cells, subsidiary cells, and epidermal hairs (trichomes).
Role: Protection against water loss, regulation of gas exchange, secretion, water and mineral absorption

89. Optical Microscopes (page 118)
1. (a) Eyepiece lens
    (b) Arm
    (c) Coarse focus knob
    (d) Fine focus knob
    (e) Objective lens
    (f) Mechanical stage
    (g) Condenser
    (h) In-built light source
    (i) Eyepiece lens
    (j) Eyepiece focus
    (k) Focus knob
    (l) Objective lens
    (m) Stage

2. (a) 600X magnification   (b) 600X magnification

3. A compound light microscope produces a flat (2-dimensional) image, which looks through a thin, transparent sample. Dissecting microscopes produce a 3-dimensional image, which looks at the surface details.

4. (a) Dissecting   (b) Compound microscope

5. (a) Magnification is the number of times larger an object appears compared to the actual size.
    (b) Resolution is the ability to distinguish between two objects. The higher the resolution, the higher the magnification can be (and image will still be clear).

6. Steps for setting up a microscope
    1. Turn on the light source.
    2. Rotate the objective lenses until the shortest lens is in place (pointing down towards the stage). This is the lowest power objective lens.
    3. Adjust the distance between the eyepieces so that they are comfortable for your eyes.
    4. Place the slide on the microscope stage. Secure with the sample clips.
    5. Focus and centre the specimen using the low objective lens. Focus firstly with the coarse focus knob, then with the fine focus knob.
    6. Focus the eyepieces to adjust your view.
    7. Adjust the illumination to an appropriate level by adjusting the iris diaphragm and the condenser. The light should appear on the slide directly below the objective lens, and give an even amount of illumination.
    8. Fine tune the illumination so you can view maximum detail on your sample.
    9. Focus and centre the specimen using the medium objective lens. Focus firstly with the coarse focus knob, then with the fine focus knob (if needed).
    10. Focus and centre the specimen using the high objective lens. Adjust focus using the fine focus knob only.

90. Measuring and Counting Using a Microscope
(page 120)
1. 1.4×10^{-2} mm or 14 microns

2. (a) Area: 0.4 mm^2 Volume: 4×10^{-3} mm^3

    (b)

	Day 1	Day 2	Day 3
No. of cells counted	4	9	17
Cells in 5 cm^3	5.0×10^6	1.1×10^7	2.1×10^7

3. Volume of central area: $1 \times 1 \times 0.1 = 0.1$ mm^3 = 0.0001 cm^3.
    $3 \div 0.000\,1 = 30\,000$. $30\,000 \times 6 = 180\,000$.
    $180\,000 \div 8 = 22\,500 = 2.25 \times 10^4$ pollen grains per anther.

91. Calculating Linear Magnification (page 121)
1. Actual size = image size ÷ magnification
    = $52\,000$ µm ÷ 140
    = 400 µm (0.4 mm)

2. (a) Actual length of scale line = 10 mm
        Given length of scale line = 0.5 mm
        $10 \div 0.5 = 20$ x magnification

    (b) Measured length = 42 mm
        Magnification = 20 x
        Actual length = $42 \div 20 = 2.1$ mm

3. 43 mm = $43\,000$ µm
    Magnification = size of the image ÷ actual size of object
    = $43\,000$ µm ÷ 2 µm
    = $21\,500$ x   magnification.

92. Preparing a Slide (page 122)
1. Thin sections allow light to pass through so features can be more easily seen. Thin sections also reduce the layers of cells (making it easier to see details).

2. The coverslip helps to smooth out the specimen and exclude air bubbles that may obscured features.

3. The onion epidermal cells do not take part in photosynthesis, so they do not contain chloroplasts.

4. Low magnification allows a larger area of the slide to be viewed, allowing specific areas to be located more easily. It also makes focussing easier and protects the slide and lens from damage caused by large movements during coarse focussing.

93. Staining a Slide (page 123)
1. Stains are mostly used to enhance specific features of a sample (e.g. specific organelles).

2. Viable stains are harmless and can be used on living samples. Non-viable staining is used on cell or tissue preparations which are dead.

3. (a) Trypan blue
    (b) Iodine solution
    (c) Aniline sulfate
    (d) Methylene blue

94. Practising Biological Drawings (page 124)
1. Students own work. Red blood cells are the most numerous. Neutrophils should be the most numerous white blood cells.

95. Electron Microscopes (page 125)
1. The limit of resolution is related to wavelength (about 0.45X the wavelength). The shortest visible light has a wavelength of about 450 nm giving a resolution of 0.45 x 450 nm; close to 200 nm. Points less than 200 nm apart will be perceived as one point or a blur. Electron beams have a shorter wavelength than light so the resolution is much greater (points 0.5 nm apart can be distinguished as separate points; a resolving power that is 400X that of a light microscope).

2. (a) **SEM**: A scanning EM will show the surface features of cells in great detail, which is useful for identification because pollen species have unique surface features. A LM would not provide sufficient detail and TEMs are used for sections, not surface details.
    (b) **TEM**: The very thin sections and high resolution achievable with a transmission EM can reveal the fine ultrastructure of an organelle. A LM would not provide enough magnification nor resolution.
    (c) **Compound light microscope**: A blood cell count requires sufficient magnification to distinguish cell types while retaining an ability to see a large number of cells at once.
    (d) **Dissecting microscope**: A dissecting microscope is the only choice for examining a living organism of this size

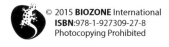
© 2015 **BIOZONE** International
ISBN: 978-1-927309-27-8
Photocopying Prohibited

(1 mm) that must be kept restrained in water while being observed. It increases the magnification enough to view the animal's organs through the transparent carapace.

3. A TEM   E SEM
    B Compound LM   F Compound LM
    C TEM   G Dissecting LM
    D Compound LM   H SEM

96. Viruses (page 127)

1. Viruses are acellular, they have no metabolism by themselves and therefore require living cells in order to replicate.

2. In general a virus is composed of a protein coat surrounding nuclear material (DNA or RNA). All have some means of recognising and interacting with a host cell in order to infect it (e.g. tail fibres or glycoprotein spikes).

3. (a) Glycoprotein spikes enable the virus attach to a host cell.
    (b) Tail fibres enable the phage to attach to a host cell.
    (c) The protein capsid encloses the genetic material and prevent it from immediate degradation inside the host.

97. Life Cycle of a Bacteriophage (page 128)

1. The lytic cycle is characterised by multiplication of the virus and lysis of the cell. The lysogenic cycle is characterised by integration into the host chromosome and cycles of nucleic acid replication (no host cell lysis).
Summary detail for reference:
Lytic cycle
– The virus (or phage) attaches itself to the host cell and inserts its DNA and some enzymes.
– Virus induces transcription of its own genes and uses cellular machinery to express those genes (produce the viral components).
– Viral components are assembled and the new (replicated) viruses burst out of the cell (cell lysis).

Lysogenic cycle
– The phage attaches to the host cell and inserts its nucleic acid and some enzymes into the host cell.
– Viral nucleic acid integrates into the host DNA.
– Viral nucleic acid is replicated (reproduced) along with that of the host cell. This occurs indefinitely until the virus is induced to enter the lytic cycle.

2. Within the lysogenic cycle, the bacterial cell may develop new properties with the integration of its DNA with phage DNA.

98. Life Cycle of a Retrovirus (page 129)

1. (a) HIV enters a T cell by attaching to the CD4 receptors on the cell surface, and fusing with the cell's plasma membrane.
    (b) Reverse transcriptase transcribes the viral RNA into viral DNA. This must occur for the viral genes to be able to integrate into the host's chromosomes where it stays as a provirus.
    (c) The provirus remains integrated with the host's chromosome and persists as a latent infection. This means that it can reinfect new host cells whenever the DNA is replicated.

2. (a) Retroviruses integrate their genetic material into the host's own chromosome, so their latency protects them from drugs that target actively replicating viral particles.
    (b) Without revere transcriptase, the viral RNA cannot be transcribed into viral DNA and it can neither integrate into the host's chromosome nor use the host cell's enzymes to transcribe its genes.

99. Antiviral Drugs (page 130)

1. (a) Blocking receptor binding prevents the virus engaging with receptors on the cell surface and so stops it from entering or injecting DNA into the cell.
    (b) Inhibiting assembly stops the cell from producing new virions and the replication cycle is stopped.

2. A combination of drugs can target all stages of the viral life cycle making removing the infection far more likely. It also reduces the chance that the therapy will fail because of a resistance to any one drug.

100 Controlling Viral Disease (page 131)

1. Factors in creasing the risk of spread between countries include international trade (infected goods or livestock) and international, rapid (e.g. air) travel.

2. Ebola spreads by contact with bodily fluids e.g. blood.

3. Ebola is more common because larger numbers of people are moving into areas were the reservoir is found, increasing the likelihood of infection.

4 (a) The infectious agent or pathogen, e.g. *Ebolavirus*.
    (b) Where the infectious agent is naturally found, e.g. fruit bats.
    (c) How the infectious agent leaves the reservoir, e.g. through the bush meat trade or a bite.
    (d) How the infectious agent is transmitted between people. For Ebola, this is by contact with bodily fluids.
    (e) The way the infectious agent enters the host. Ebola enters through wounds or mucous membranes.
    (f) Whether or not the host is open to contracting the disease (i.e. not immune). Susceptibility describes how easily a host is infected. Cramped living conditions, lack of health education, and poor sanitation increase risk of infection.

5. Student's response based on the points given in the activity.

101. Cell Division (page 133)

1. (a) Mitosis occurs in body cells (somatic cells) in animals.
    (b) Mitosis is responsible for growth of an organism, repair and replacement of damaged cells, and for asexual reproduction in some eukaryotes.

2. (a) Meiosis occurs in sex organs (testes and ovaries) in animals.
    (b) It produces sex cells (gametes) for the purposes of sexual reproduction.

3. Gametes are haploid (N) because meiosis halves the chromosome number of a somatic cell. Fusion of gametes in fertilisation restores the diploid number for the organism (2N).

102. Mitosis and the Cell Cycle (page 134)

1. The function of mitosis is growth and repair of the body. It may also allow asexual reproduction in some organisms.

2. The DNA must replicate (during S phase).

3. (a) Interphase: The stage between cell divisions (mitoses). Just before mitosis, the DNA is replicated to form an extra copy of each chromosome (still part of the same chromosome as an extra chromatid).
    (b) Mitosis: Homologous chromatids separate. The nucleus divides in two, each new nucleus containing a set of chromosomes.
    (c) Cytokinesis: The cytoplasm divides in two, forming two new cells.

4. Cytokinesis in animal cells involves the formation of a contractile ring of microtubules that constrict to cleave the cell. In plant cell cytokinesis, vesicles deliver cell wall a material to the middle of the cell where a cell plate (a precursor to the new cell wall) forms. The vesicles coalesce to form the plasma membranes of the new cell surfaces.

103. Recognising Stages in Mitosis (page 136)

1. (a) Anaphase
    (b) Prophase
    (c) Metaphase
    (d) Telophase

2. (a) Estimate below. This calculation is based on seeing enough of the cell's nucleus. Cells in cytokinesis were included in interphase (not in mitosis).

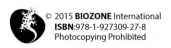

Stage	No. of cells	% of total cells	Estimated time in stage
Interphase	47	41.5	9 h 57 min
Mitosis	66	58.6	14 h 03 min
Total	113	100	24 hours

(b) 66/113 = 0.58

3. The mitotic index will decrease.

104. Regulation of the Cell Cycle (page 137)

1. Cell cycle check points ensure that the cell has the required resources and has met the required conditions to successfully complete the next phase of the cell cycle.

2. (a) The metaphase checkpoint ensures all the chromatids are attached to the spindle and under the proper tension.
   (b) It ensures all daughter cells end up with the correct chromosome complement. Only when all the chromatids are properly attached can the cell proceed to anaphase, in which the chromatids are pulled apart.

3. If the cell cycle was not regulated cells would go into uncontrolled cell division, resulting in the formation of tumours. Cycle regulation also ensures that the cell reaches the appropriate size and volume to divide successfully.

105. Meiosis (page 138)

1. In the first division of meiosis, homologous pairs of chromosomes pair to form bivalents. Segments of chromosome may be exchanged in crossing over and the homologues then separate (are pulled apart). This division reduces the number of chromosomes in the intermediate cells, so that only one chromosome from each homologous pair is present.

2. In the second division of meiosis, chromatids separate (are pulled apart), but the number of chromosomes stays the same. This is more or less a 'mitotic' division.

3. (a) DNA replication occurs in interphase.
   (b) A chromosome is a single piece of coiled, condensed DNA. A chromatid is one half of a replicated chromosome (held to its other chromatid at the centromere).

4. (a) A haploid cell has only one set of chromosomes. A diploid cell has two sets of chromosomes.
   (b) The haploid cells are at the bottom (the gametes).

5. (a) ABCD   (c) abcD
   (b) ABCd   (d) abcd

6. (a) Unexpected combinations of alleles for genes will be present in gametes (recombinants).
   (b) The offspring are more genetically variable than they would otherwise be.

106. Crossing Over Problems (page 140)

Each problem stands alone (they are not a sequence).

1. (a) Gene sequences after crossing over at point 2:

   (b) A, B and C

2. (a) Gene sequences after crossing over at points 6 & 7:

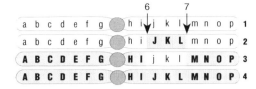

   (b) J, K and L

3. (a) Gene sequences after crossing over at points 1 and 3, 5 and 7. (Note that results for chromatids 2 & 3 are interchangeable):

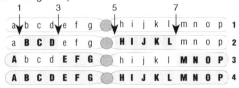

   (b) B, C, D and H, I, J, K, L

4. Genes on one chromosome would be inherited together and there would be less variation in the gametes and therefore in the offspring. Variation would arise only from mutation and from the combination of maternal and paternal gametes at fertilisation.

107. Modelling Meiosis (page 141)

The genotype/phenotype of the offspring that students obtain will depend on their own phenotypes.

108. Mitosis vs Meiosis (page 143)

1. Mitosis involves a division of the chromatids into two new daughter cells thus maintaining the original number of chromosomes in the parent cell. Meiosis involves a division of the homologous pairs of chromosomes into two intermediary daughter cells thus reducing the diploid number by half. The second stage of meiosis is similar to a mitotic division, but the haploid number is maintained because the chromatids separate.

2. The first meiotic division is a reduction division, halving the number of chromosomes. The second division is a 'mitotic' type division, the chromatids are separated but the number of chromosomes remain the same.

3. The processes of recombination and independent assortment of the chromosomes during meiosis sort alleles into different combinations and thus introduces genetic diversity.

109. Chromosome Mutations (page 144)

1. (b) Original sequence: ABCDEFGHMNOPQRST
       Mutated sequence: AB**FEDC**GHMNOPQRST
   (c) Original sequences: 1234567890
       ABCDEFGHMNOPQRST
       Mutated sequences: **ABCDEF**1234567890
       GHMNOPQRST
   (d) Original sequences: ABCDEFMNOPQ
       ABCDEFMNOPQ
       Mutated sequences: **ABCDE**ABCDEFMNOPQ
       FMNOPQ

2. Inversion, because there is no **immediate** loss of genes from the chromosome. (At a later time, inverted genes may be lost from a chromosome during crossing over, due to unequal exchange of segments).

110. Non-Disjunction in Meiosis (page 145)

1. Non-disjunction results in abnormal gamete numbers in some gametes. As a result, certain phenotypic traits are exhibited (e.g. facial features, mental retardation). Certain metabolic processes may also be affected.

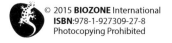

2. Non-disjunction in the parental cell during meiosis I results in both the daughter cells being faulty which will be transferred to the daughter cells produced in meiosis II. Nondisjunction in a parental cell during meiosis II results in only half the total number of daughter cells being faulty.

3. The maternal age effect refers to an increased risk of chromosome abnormalities with advancing maternal age. The risk of aneuploidies, such as Down syndrome, increase with every year a women ages.

111. Aneuploidy in Humans (page 146)

1. Embryos from left to right: XXY, XO, XXY, XO.

2. (a) Trisomic female (metafemale or superfemale)
   (b) Klinefelter syndrome
   (c) Turner syndrome

3. The YO configuration has no X chromosome (the X contains essential genes not found on the Y).

4. (a) For karyotype A: (circle X chromosome)
      Chromosome configuration: 45, X (44 + X)
      Sex: female
      Syndrome: Turner
   (b) For karyotype B: (circle XXY chromosomes)
      Chromosome configuration: 47, XXY (44 + XXY),
      Sex: male
      Syndrome: Klinefelter

5. Number of Barr bodies:
   (a) Jacob syndrome: 0
   (b) Klinefelter syndrome: 1
   (c) Turner syndrome: 0

6. X chromosome inactivation ensures that the proteins encoded by the genes on the X chromosome will only be produced by the one active copy.

7. (a) **Nullisomy**: 0, both of a pair of homologous chromosomes are missing.
   (b) **Monosomy**: 1, one chromosome appears instead of the normal two.
   (c) **Trisomy**: 3, three chromosomes appear instead of two, the result of faulty meiosis.
   (d) **Polysomy**: 3+, the condition in which one or more chromosomes are represented more than twice in the cell (includes trisomy).

112. Gametes (page 148)

1. Once deposited in the vagina, sperm must be able to move through the uterus and into the oviducts to reach and fertilise the ovum. Sperm only live for about 48 hours, so they must be able to move quickly to reach the ovum to attempt fertilisation before they die.

2. (a) Ova move as a result of the wave-like motion of the cilia in the Fallopian tube.
   (b) Ova must be larger than sperm because they must contain nutritional resources to support the early development of the embryo.

3. The sperm is a motile cell, requiring propulsion to reach the ovum in order to fertilise it. Energy for movement (ATP) is provided by cellular respiration in the large number of mitochondria present in the sperm cell.

113. Spermatogenesis (page 149)

1. (a) Spermatogenesis
   (b) Testis
   (c) Four
   (d) Meiosis

2. LH stimulates synthesis and secretion of testosterone which is required for sperm production. FSH supports the Sertoli cells and sperm maturation.

3. About 100-400 million sperm are needed because only a very small percentage of them eventually reach the ovum (remember that the sperm must negotiate the cervix and then find their way into the Fallopian tube). Note: Although

only one sperm fertilizes the egg, the combined action of the enzymes from a large number of sperm is needed in order to help digest the jelly-like barrier around the egg.

114. Oogenesis (page 150)

1. (a) Oogenesis
   (b) In the ovarian follicle within the ovary

2. Sperm are continually produced within the testes from puberty onwards. One spermatogonium produces four identical mature sperm. Many millions of sperm are produced every day. In contrast, a female is born with her full complement of eggs, which develop in stages. The eggs begin to mature from puberty. One egg matures and is released at every menstrual cycle until menopause is reached. Only one mature ovum is produced from an oogonium.

3. Males continue to produce new sperm throughout their reproductive life span. Because the sperm are newly produced, a higher proportion are genetically viable and healthy. Females are born with their full complement of immature eggs. As a female ages so do the eggs, so egg viability declines with age. Oogenesis eventually ceases at menopause.

115. Fertilisation and Early Growth (page 151)

1. (a) Capacitation: Changes in the surface of the sperm cell (caused by the acid environment of the vagina) that make possible its adhesion to the oocyte.
   (b) Acrosome reaction: The release of enzymes from the acrosome at the head of the sperm. These enzymes digest a pathway through the follicle cells and the zona pellucida.
   (c) Fusion of egg and sperm membranes: Enables the sperm nucleus to enter the egg. The fusion causes a sudden depolarisation of the membrane that forms a fast block to further sperm entry.
   (d) Cortical reaction: A permanent change in the egg surface that provides a slow (permanent) block to sperm entry. Involves the release of cortical granules into the perivitelline space, followed by the release of substances from the granules that raise and harden the vitelline layer.
   (e) Fusion of egg and sperm nuclei: The fusion of nuclei forms the diploid zygote and initiates the rapid cell division that follows fertilisation.

2. It is necessary to prevent fertilisation of the egg by more than one sperm because this would result in too many chromosomes in the zygote (making the zygote non-viable or unable to survive). Note: Triploidy (a condition resulting from two sperm fertilising an egg) is frequently found among spontaneous miscarriages.

3. (a) The oocyte is arrested in metaphase of meiosis II after it has undergone the first meiotic division.
   (b) Meiotic division proceeds to completion if the egg is fertilised (i.e. fertilisation triggers completion).

4. (a) Zygote nucleus: Sperm: 50%,   Egg: 50%
   (b) Zygote cytoplasm: Sperm: 0%,   Egg: 100%

5. Cleavage is the rapid early cell division of the fertilised egg to produce the ball of cells that will become the blastocyst. Cleavage increases the number of cells but not the size of the zygote.

6. (a) Implantation of the blastocyst is important for establishing the close contact between the developing fetus and the uterine lining. The uterine lining can then provide for the early nourishment of the embryo.
   (b) HCG prevents degeneration of the corpus luteum, so that it continues to secrete progesterone and maintain the pregnancy (placenta takes over this role at 12 weeks).

7. This the period during which most organ development occurs and the developing tissues are most prone to the damaging effects of drugs.

© 2015 **BIOZONE** International
ISBN:978-1-927309-27-8
Photocopying Prohibited

116. Reproduction in Plants (page 153)

1. Plants alternate between a diploid sporophyte generation (which produces haploid spores by meiosis) and a haploid gametophyte generation (which produces the haploid gametes by mitosis).

2. (a) Sporophyte: A tree, shrub or flower, e.g. pine, tulip, fern, oak.
   (b) Gametophyte: pollen, prothallus in fern plants.

3. **Spores**
   Produced by: Sporophyte
   Process: Meiosis
   Gametes
   Produced by: Gametophyte
   Process: Mitosis
   Zygote:
   Produced by: Gametes
   Process: Fertilisation

117. Reproduction in Angiosperms (page 154)

1. Note: The diagram is simplified. Step c (meiosis) produces microscopes (N) which give rise to the gametophyte by mitosis. The haploid microscopes (and megaspores) have not been indicated on the diagram. This is somewhat misleading and has been since clarified.

   (a) 2N   (d) Fertilisation
   (b) N   (e) Mitosis
   (c) Meiosis

2. (a) The anther.   (b) The ovule.

3. Pollen may be transferred to the stigma by wind or pollinating animals, such as insects.

4. One sperm nucleus and two polar nuclei.

5. Triploid.

6. The sperm nuclei reach the egg cell via the pollen tube

118. Pollination and Fertilisation (page 155)

1. (a) The microspore mother cell produces the haploid microspores by meiosis, which give rise to the haploid gametophytes (pollen grains) by mitosis.
   (b) 4

2. (a) The megaspore mother cell produces the haploid megaspores by meiosis, which give rise to the egg cell and the polar nuclei by mitosis.
   (b) 1

3. The generative cell produces two sperm nuclei.

4. The pollen tube enters the ovule through the micropyle

5. Limiting self pollination prevents the negative effects of inbreeding and increases variability and therefore adaptability in a changing environment.

6. Calcium.

7. (a)-(c) any of the following in any order:
   – Male and female flowers on different plants.
   – Physically separating the male and female parts in the same flower.
   – Different maturation times for male and female gametes.
   – Gametes from the same plant incompatible.

8. **Pollination** refers specifically to the transfer of pollen from the male anthers to the female stigma. **Fertilisation** in plants refers to formation of the embryo by the fusion of a sperm nucleus with the egg.

9. The double fertilisation results in the formation of both the embryo and the endosperm (food store). This is different from gymnosperms in which the second sperm cell degenerates.

10. Most ovaries contain many ovules.

119. Sucrose Concentration and Pollen Tube Growth (page 157)

1.

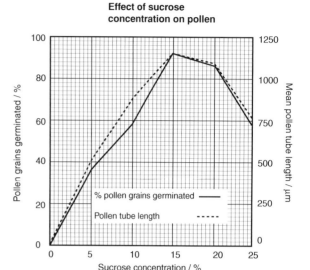

Effect of sucrose concentration on pollen

Legend:
% pollen grains germinated ——
Pollen tube length - - - - -

x-axis: Sucrose concentration / %
left y-axis: Pollen grains germinated / %
right y-axis: Mean pollen tube length / μm

2.

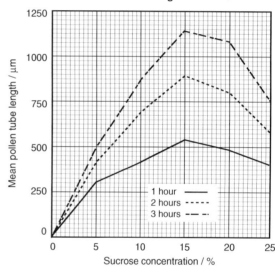

Pollen tube length over time

Legend:
1 hour ——
2 hours - - - -
3 hours –– –

x-axis: Sucrose concentration / %
y-axis: Mean pollen tube length / μm

3. (a) 15%   (b) 15%

4. Borate prevents the pollen grains from bursting.

120. Chapter Review (page 158)

No model answer. Summary is the student's own.

121. KEY TERMS: Mix and Match (page 160)

1. (a)

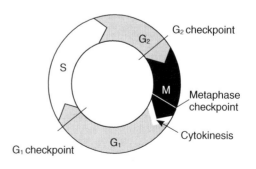

Labels: G_2 checkpoint, Metaphase checkpoint, Cytokinesis, G_1 checkpoint
Cycle segments: G_2, S, M, G_1

   (b) G_1: Cell grows and develops

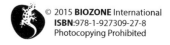
© 2015 **BIOZONE** International
ISBN:978-1-927309-27-8
Photocopying Prohibited

G₂: Cell continues to grow. Chromosomes begin condensing.
M phase: Mitosis. The nucleus divides.
S Phase: DNA synthesis. The chromosomes replicate.

2. (a) Crossing over
   (b) Meiosis
   (c) Prophase I.

3. cell cycle (E), cell wall (G), cell division (C), endosperm (I), fertilisation (K), interphase (A), latency (L), meiosis (J), mitosis (B), organelle (D), pollination (H), virus (F)

4. (a) Mitochondrion
   (b) Both plant and animal cell
   (c) Chloroplast
   (d) Plant cell

122. Classification System (page 162)

1. (a) 2. Kingdom   (b) 2. Animal
       3. Phylum   3. Chordata
       4. Class   4. Mammalia
       5. Order   5. Primates
       6. Family (given)   6. Hominidae (given)
       7. Genus   7. *Homo*
       8. Species   8. *sapiens*

2. There are many possibilities. Common examples are:
   Keep **P**ond **C**lean **O**r **F**roggy **G**ets **S**ick
   Kids **P**laying **C**ricket **O**r **F**ootball **G**et **S**marter

3. *Panthera tigris tigris*

4. (a) Binomial nomenclature
   (b) Genus and species (generic and specific name).

5. (a) and (b) in any order:
   (1) Avoid confusion over the use of common names for organisms, (2) provide a unique name for each type of organism, (3) attempt to determine/define the evolutionary relationship of organisms (phylogeny).

123 How Do We Assign Species? (page 164)

1. Traditional methods of classification use morphology to distinguish species. However some species (e.g. mimics or cryptic species) can look alike but have very different genetics. This can lead to misclassification.

2. Species complexes and cryptic species means that conservation efforts need to be more wider ranging than they might otherwise have been in order to include all possible members of the species complex.

124. The Biological Species Concept (page 165)

1. Behavioural (they show no interest in each other).

2. Physical barrier; sea separating Australia from SE Asia.

3. The red wolf is rare and may have difficulty finding another member of its species to mate with.

4. The populations on the two land masses, which have identical appearance and habitat requirements, were connected relatively recently by a land bridge during the last ice age (about 18 000 years ago). This would have permitted breeding between the populations. Individuals from the current populations have been brought together and are able to interbreed and produce fertile offspring.

5. Several definitions of a biological species are possible. Most simply, a species is the lowest taxonomic grouping of organisms. From a functional point of view, a species is a group of organisms that are freely interbreeding (or potentially so) but reproductively isolated from other such groups. Species are usually (but now not exclusively) recognised by their morphological characters. Cryptic species are morphologically indistinguishable, but reproductively isolated as a result of behavioural or other differences. 'Species' that do not reproduce sexually (with the combination of gametes) at any stage provide problems for a standard species definition. Such organisms include bacteria, where genera

and 'species' are distinguished on the basis of structure and metabolism. In these cases, the species could more correctly said to be types or strains.

125. The Phylogenetic Species Concept (page 166)

1. (a) Under the PSC, species are assigned on the basis of shared derived characteristics, which may be morphological or biochemical. A species is the smallest group that all share a derived character state.
   (b) Problems (one of):
       It can lead to a proliferation of species that are difficult to distinguish.
       It is difficult to justify its application to morphologically distinct but interbreeding populations.
   (c) The PSC might be more appropriate than the BSC for extinct organisms, and for asexually reproducing organisms such as bacteria.

2. Genetic techniques can be used to trace the occurrence of new character states and distinguish species on the basis of a unique combination of characters. Taxa that share more derived characters are more closely related than those that share fewer. This produces a hierarchy of shared character states, which leads to a tree of relatedness.

126. Gel Electrophoresis (page 167)

1. Purpose: To separate mixtures of molecules (proteins, nucleic acids) on the basis of size, electric charge and other physical properties.

2. (a) The frictional (retarding) force of each fragment's size (larger fragments travel more slowly than smaller ones).
   (b) The strength of the electric field (movement is more rapid in a stronger field). **Note**: The temperature and ionic strength of the buffer can be varied to optimise separation of the fragments.

3. The gel is full of pores (holes) through which the fragments must pass. Smaller fragments pass through these pores more easily than larger ones.

127. The Principles of DNA Sequencing (page 168)

1. (a) A dideoxyribonucleic acid
   (b) and (c)

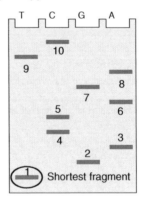

   (d) T G A C C A G A T C
   (e) A C T G G T C T A G

2. A reaction vessel is needed for each modified base. If all the modified bases were put in the same vessel there would be no way of distinguishing between them once placed on an electrophoresis gel.

3. 1% modified DNA is enough to produced terminated DNA fragments but is a small enough to allow other non-modified DNA to be incorporated in the DNA fragment. Too much modified DNA would cause termination of DNA replication too early in too many cases.

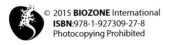

128. Distinguishing Species by Gel Electrophoresis
(page 169)
1. (a) and (b)

Cow synthesised DNA:
TGATTGTAAGCTTTCAGGGTGGGTGATTA
Cow sample DNA:
ACTAACATTCGAAAGTCCCACCCACTAAT

Sheep synthesised DNA:
TAGTTGTAGGCTTTTTGGGTGGGTGATTA
Sheep sample DNA:
ATCAACATCCGAAAAACCCACCCACTAAT

Goat synthesised DNA:
TGGTTGTAGGCTTTCTGGGTGGGTAATTA
Goat sample DNA:
ACCAACATCCGAAAGACCCACCCATTAAT

Horse synthesised DNA:
TGTTTGTAGGCCTTTAGAGTGGGTGATTA
Horse sample DNA:
ACAAACATCCGGAAATCTCACCCACTAAT

(c) Sheep and goat (3 differences)
(d) Goat and horse (6 differences)

2.

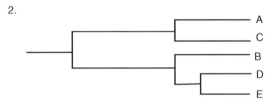

A
C
B
D
E

129. Bioinformatics (page 170)
1. Bioinformatics has allowed scientists to store and quickly access and analyse many different DNA sequences. This has lead to greater understanding of evolutionary relationships.

2. (a) Hippopotamuses
(b)

Hippopotamuses
Toothed whales
Baleen whales

(c) Evidence shows pigs branched off much earlier and are related to peccaries

130. Using DNA Probes (page 171)
1. A DNA probe allows a region of DNA to be marked and identified.

2. The DNA probe is a sequence of DNA that is complementary to the target region of DNA. It is therefore able to bond to the target DNA allowing that region to be identified.

3. Double stranded DNA must be denatured to a single strand so that the base pairs are exposed and the complementary base pairs on the DNA probe can bond to the target region.

4. Genes are visualised using fluorescent light or X-ray film, depending on the tag that has been added to the probe being used. The target DNA sequence will appear as a band on the electrophoresis gel.

131. Investigating Genetic Diversity (page 172)
1. The TV11-14 group forms a distinct clade, which branched before the genetically distinct TV1-10 group (which is part of another clade that includes the Cape Royds, Cape Evans, and Beaufort Island groups). The TV1-10 group forms a cluster that is genetically closer than the other groups in the clade with which it shares a common ancestor.

2. The fact that the two types do not interbreed is significant because it means that reproductive isolating mechanisms have developed, or are in the process of developing. The two types may already be distinct species, or they could be in the process of diverging (if physical separation of the groups is

the primary factor preventing their interbreeding).

3. Gene flow (interbreeding) between populations will be very limited, if it occurs at all, because the springtails have very limited motility and are likely to die if blown any distance.

4. These conditions would have been ideal for the development of two species from a common ancestor. Small populations, isolated on mountain tops on either side of the valley, are likely to have had slight genetic differences and may then have been subjected to subtly different selection pressures (different microclimates etc.). The low dispersal (lack of gene flow) combined with the small population size, would have increased the differences between the isolated populations, which could then diverge genetically in a relatively short time.

132. Validating New Evidence (page 174)
1. The peer review process uses experts in a particular scientific field to validate new research. It ensures that good methodology has been used, and that the results and conclusions are valid and appropriate.

2. Data that is not peer reviewed has not be checked for potential inaccuracies, false claims, or bias These can cause people in the public to believe certain things are true when they are not.

3. In the more than 150 years since the publication of Darwin's theory, a huge body of evidence has been presented to test and give depth to our understanding of the mechanisms of evolution. The data, both experimental and observational, has been rigorously reviewed, discussed, and tested by peers in the respective fields. Overwhelmingly, the result of this work has been a validation of Darwin's original ideas, albeit modified in the light of our greater understanding of molecular genetics.

133. Classification Systems: The Old and the New
(page 175)
1. (a) DNA sequencing evidence supports splitting the former taxon of Monera into the two domains, Bacteria and Archaea. The DNA indicates that the differences between these two taxa are as great as the differences between the prokaryotes and eukaryotes, which represent the third domain of life.
(b) The five kingdom classification is biased towards multicellular organisms and does not take into account the large differences between single celled organisms nor the metabolic and sequence similarities between the eukaryotes and Archeans.
(c) Molecular evidence has helped to separate groups that were once grouped together on the basis of appearance and to find new evolutionary relationships between groups.

2. Molecular evidence provides comparisons of the hereditary material and how it has changed from species to species. Species with similar appearances (e.g. mimics) can be difficult to distinguish and similarities may be unrelated to ancestry. Moreover, molecular evidence removes the bias inherent in assumptions, e.g. in the past, people assumed that chimpanzees must be more closely related to other apes than to humans, but molecular evidence shows this to be untrue.

3. Evidence based on genetic differences.

134. Constructing Cladograms (page 177)
1. (a) A shared derived characteristic is a characteristic that is shared by two or more closely related groups and originated in their common ancestor. A shared ancestral characteristic is one that arises in a taxon that is ancestral to more than one group (e.g. backbones are ancestral in mammals and reptiles).
(b) Ancestral characteristics are not very useful in constructing phylogenies because they cause very distantly related groups to be placed together, i.e. they don't provide enough information to separate closely related taxa.

2. Parsimony assumes that the cladogram with the least number

© 2015 **BIOZONE** International
ISBN:978-1-927309-27-8
Photocopying Prohibited

of steps is the correct one.

3. (a) Question bettwe phrased as "What is the advantage of using DNA analysis over morphological comparisons to construct a cladogram?"
   Some species can be morphologically similar and can therefore be very difficult to distinguish. The similarity may be the result of adaptation to similar environments (selection pressures) and not the result of common ancestry. DNA analysis shows the evolutionary relationships in terms of DNA changes over time.
   (b) Conserved DNA sequences are unlikely to have many mutations (as these are likely to be fatal) and the mutations that are found in them are likely to be important divergence points in evolution (evolutionarily significant). Therefore analysis of DNA differences will provide a more accurate evolutionary relationship between species.

4. (a) Data match 5. The mutation from C to T must have occurred separately in pig and whale/hippo ancestors.
   (b) Cattle do not have the mutation but have most of the other mutations that whales and hippos do. Therefor either this mutations happen twice (in pigs and whale/hippos) after the ancestral split or it happen at the ancestral split and then cattle mutated back to the original C base at the cattle/ whale and hippo split.

6. The phylogenetic tree can be tested by constructing trees based on a wide variety of characteristics (i.e. molecular and morphological) and/or using various phylogenetic methods. Trees obtained using different methodologies and different data are all likely to agree if the phylogeny is correct.

   Teacher's note: A typical phylogenetic analysis involves many decisions, including what type of data to sample, what phylogenetic method to apply, whether or not to order or weight characters, and which taxa and characters to include or exclude. Different choices can lead to very different trees. In practice, computer simulations, statistical analyses (such as bootstrap analysis) and agreement between trees from different data sets are all used to test proposed phylogenetic trees. Students should be aware that cladistic analysis is only one method for constructing a phylogenetic tree.

135. Mechanism of Natural Selection (page 179)

1. 1) Overproduction of the population, 2) genetic variation in the population, 3) competition for resources and survival of those with more favourable variations (natural selection), 4) inheritance of favourable variations and proliferation of individuals with these variations.

2. Mutations (creates new alleles) and sexual reproduction (produces new combinations of alleles).

3. The changes in the inherited characteristics of a population over many generations.

4. A population produces more offspring than will survive to reproduce. There is genetic variation in the offspring. Some of this variation will result in offspring phenotypes that are more suited to the prevailing environment than others. Competition will select for favourable phenotypes. The genetic component of the variation will be inherited by the next generation so that proportionally more of the favourable phenotype will be present in the next generation of offspring. Over time, favourable phenotypes will proliferate and unfavourable phenotypes will become rare or disappear.

5.

Beetle population	% Brown beetle	% Red beetles	% Red beetles with spots
1	86.7	6.7	6.7
2	46.6	33.3	20
3	20	46.7	33.3

136. What is Adaptation? (page 181)

Note rhino photo labels mistakenly transposed (since corrected).

1. Adaptive features are genetically determined traits that have a function to the organism in its environment. Acclimatisation refers to the changes made by an organism during its lifetime to environmental conditions (note that some adaptive features do involve changes in physiology).

2. Shorter extremities are associated with colder climates, whereas elongated extremities are associated with warmer climates. The differences are associated with heat conservation (shorter limbs/ears lose less heat to the environment).

3. Large body sizes conserve more heat and have more heat producing mass relative to the surface area over which heat can be lost.

137. Adaptation and Niche (page 182)

For each of the following the list is not exhaustive, but uses examples given on the diagrams. Note that most adaptations have components of structure, physiology, and behaviour (e.g. threat behaviours involve use of structural features. Thermoregulatory physiology involves some behaviour etc.). Categories may not be mutually exclusive.

1. (a) **Structural**: Generally these are adaptations to aid efficient digging and tunnelling, assisting survival though protection and effective food gathering. Clawed hindfeet push soil out of the way when digging (improves efficiency). External ear openings are covered by fur to protect them when digging. Short, powerful limbs with efficient lever arrangement of muscles and joints aids rotation-thrust movement in digging. Forefeet powerfully clawed as digging tools. Velvety fur reduces friction when moving through the soil. Fur can lie in either direction so backward movement in tunnel is not hampered. Tubular body shape aids movement underground. Heavily buttressed head and neck makes tunnelling easier and more energy efficient.
   (b) **Physiological**: Well developed chemical sense aids location of food. Good sense of hearing.
   (c) **Behavioural**: Solitary and territorial behaviour (except when breeding) helps to maintain a viable food supply and reduce aggressive encounters. Sleep and feed underground offering effective protection from predators.

2. **Snow bunting** adaptations:
   (a) **Structural**: Large amount of white plumage reduces heat loss, white feathers are hollow and air filled (acting as good insulators).
   (b) **Physiological**: Lay one or two more eggs than (ecologically) equivalent species further south producing larger broods (improving breeding success), rapid moult to winter plumage is suited to the rapid seasonal changes of the Arctic.
   (c) **Behavioural**: Feeding activity continues almost uninterrupted during prolonged daylight hours (allowing large broods to be raised and improving survival and breeding success), migration to overwintering regions during Arctic winter (escapes harsh Arctic winter), will burrow into snow drifts for shelter (withstand short periods of very bad weather), males assist in brood rearing (improved breeding success).

3. (a)-(f), any six of:

   S Long, mobile ears provide acute detection of sounds from many angles (for predator detection).
   S Long, strong hind legs are adapted for rapid running (for escape from predators).
   S Cryptic/camouflage colouring of fur assists in avoiding being detected by predators.
   S Limb structure facilitates burrowing behaviour.
   P High metabolic rate and activity allows rapid response to dangers.
   P Keen sense of smell enables detection of potential threats from predators and from rabbits from other warrens (they are highly territorial).
   P Digestive system suited for coping with microbial digestion of cellulose in the hindgut.
   B European rabbit is active during any time of the day or night, but modifies its behaviour around humans to be

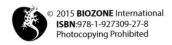

active around dusk and dawn (crepuscular).
- B Lives in groups of highly organised social structure (cooperative defence) and reduced competition between rabbits of the same warren.
- B Burrows into ground to provide nesting sites, and shelter from physical conditions and predators.
- B Thumps the ground with hind legs to warn others in the warren of impending danger.

4. Extra detail is (italics) provided as explanation:
   (a) Structural (*larger, stouter body conserves heat*).
   (b) Physiological (*concentrated urine conserves water*).
   (c) Behavioural (*move to favourable sites*).
   (d) Physiological (*higher photosynthetic rates and water conservation*).
   (e) Structural (*reduction in water loss*).
   (f) Behavioural and physiological (*hibernation involves both a reduction in metabolic rate and the behaviour necessary to acquire more food before hibernation and to seek out an appropriate site*).
   (g) Behavioural (*increase in body temperature*).

138. Natural Selection in Pocket Mice (page 184)
1. (a) DD, Dd   (b) dd

2. See column graphs below

3. (a) The dark mice are found on the dark rocks.
   (b) Dark mice are found on the dark rocks as they blend in better, making it harder for predators to spot them. Dark mice on light rocks would be easily seen by predators. The same applies for light mice and dark rocks.
   (c) The mice at BLK and WHT do not conform to this generalisation. The mice at BLK are lighter than predicted from the lower rock reflectance and the mice at WHT are darker than predicted from the higher rock reflectance.
   (d) These mice might represent a recent migration to those areas from mostly dark or light population. There has not been enough time for the population to evolve to match their surroundings.

4. Dark colour has evolved at least twice in rock pocket mice populations.

139. Selection for Skin Colour in Humans (page 186)
1. (a) Folate is essential for healthy neural development. Note: A deficiency causes (usually fatal) neural tube defects (e.g. spina bifida).
   (b) Vitamin D is required for the absorption of dietary calcium and normal skeletal development. Note: A deficiency causes rickets in children or osteomalacia in adults. Osteomalacia in pregnancy can lead to pelvic fractures and inability to carry a pregnancy to term.

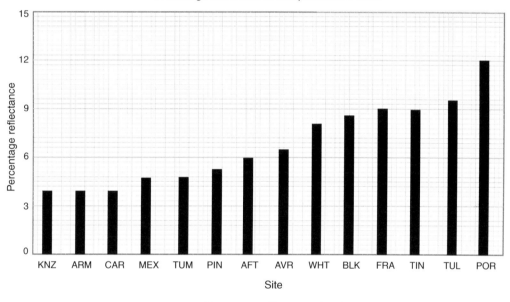

Percentage reflectance of rock pocket mice coats

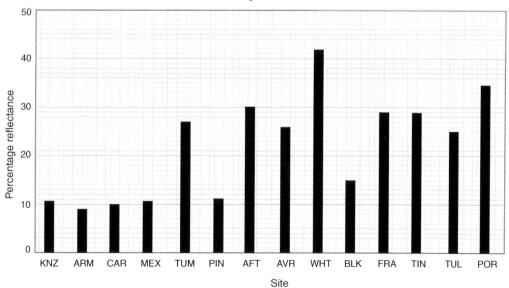

Percentage reflectance of rocks

2. (a) Skin cancer normally develops after reproductive age and therefore protection against it provides no reproductive advantage and so no mechanism for selection.
   (b) The new hypothesis for the evolution of skin colour links the skin colour-UV correlation directly to evolutionary fitness (reproductive success). Skin needs to be dark enough to protect folate stores from destruction by UV and so prevent fatal neural defects in the offspring. However it also needs to be light enough to allow enough UV to penetrate the skin on order to manufacture vitamin D for calcium absorption. Without this, the female skeleton cannot successfully support a pregnancy. Because these pressures act on individuals both before and during reproductive age they provide a mechanism for selection. The balance of opposing selective pressures determines eventual skin colouration.

3. Women have a higher requirement for calcium during pregnancy and lactation. Calcium absorption is dependent on vitamin D, making selection pressure on females for lighter skins greater than for males.

4. The Inuit people have such abundant vitamin D in their diet that the selection pressure for lighter skin (for UV absorption and vitamin D synthesis) is reduced and their skin can be darker.

5. (a) Higher chances of getting rickets or (the adult equivalent) osteomalacia due to low UV absorption.
   (b) The simplest option to avoid these problems is for these people to take dietary supplements to increase the amount of vitamin D they obtain.

140. Isolation and Species Formation (page 188)

1. Isolating mechanisms protect the gene pool from the diluting and potentially adverse effects of introduced genes. Species are well adapted to their niche; foreign genes will usually reduce fitness.

2. (a) Geographical isolation physically separates populations (and gene pools) but, if reintroduced, the two populations could potentially interbreed, i.e. reproductive isolation may not have occurred.
   (b) Geographical isolation enables populations to diverge in response to different selection pressures and (potentially) develop reproductive isolating mechanisms. Reproductive isolation won't generally occur in a populations in which there is gene flow (unless by special events such as polyploidy).

3. Geographical isolation physically separates populations (gene pools) so there is no gene flow between them. Ecological isolation arises as a result of different preferences in habitat or behaviour even though the populations occupy the same geographical area.

141. Reproductive Isolation (page 189)

1. (a) Postzygotic: hybrid breakdown
   (b) Prezygotic: structural
   (c) Prezygotic: temporal
   (d) Postzygotic: hybrid inviability

2. They are a secondary backup if the first isolating mechanism fails. The majority of species do not interbreed because of prezygotic mechanisms. Postzygotic mechanisms are generally rarer events.

142. Allopatric Speciation (page 191)

1. Animals may move into new environments to reduce competition for resources or because a new habitat becomes available (loss of geographical barrier or loss of another species).

2. Plants move by dispersing their seeds.

3. Gene flow between the parent population and dispersing populations is regular.

4. Cooler periods (glacials) result in a drop in sea level as more water is stored as ice. As the temperature increases, the ice will begin to melt, and sea level will rise. The variation in sea level will depend on how much water is stored and released in response to the temperature change.

5. (a) Physical barriers that could isolate populations include the formation of mountain ranges, the formation of rivers or their change of course, the expansion or formation of desert, the advance of ice sheets, glacial retreat (isolating alpine adapted populations), and sea level rise. On a longer time scale, the formation of seas as a result of continental drift can isolate populations too.
   (b) Emigration (leaving one area and moving to another) will potentially reduce the genetic diversity of both gene pools, the migrants and the parent population. Depending on the extent of the migration, the effect will be the same as geographical isolation. The allele frequencies of the two isolates will diverge.

6. (a) The selection pressures on an isolated population may be quite different for that of the parent population. The immediate physical environment (e.g. temperature, wind exposure) as well as climatic region (e.g. temperate to tropical) may differ, as will biotic factors, such as competition, predation, and disease. In a different region, the food type and availability is also likely to be different for the two populations. The shift in selection pressures may result in changes in allele frequencies as those best adapted to the new conditions survive to reproduce.
   (b) Some individuals in the isolated population will have allele combinations (and therefore a phenotype) that better suits the unique set of selection pressures at the new location. Over a period of time (generations) certain alleles for a gene will become more common in the gene pool, at the expense of other less suited alleles.

7. Reproductive isolation could develop in geographically isolated populations through the development of prezygotic and then postzygotic barriers to breeding. Prezygotic isolation would probably begin with ecological isolation, e.g. habitat preferences in the isolated population would diverge from the parent population in the new environment. Prezygotic isolating mechanisms that could develop subsequently to prevent successful mating include temporal isolation (e.g. seasonal shifts in the timing of breeding), incompatible behaviours (e.g. different mating rituals), and structural incompatibilities (e.g. incompatible mating apparatus). Gamete mortality (failure of egg and sperm to unite) can also prevent formation of the zygote in individuals that manage to copulate successfully. Once prezygotic isolation is established, post-zygotic mechanisms such as zygote mortality (in which the fertilised egg dies), reduced hybrid fertility, or hybrid breakdown (non-viable or sterile F2) increase the isolation of the new species and prevent gene flow between it and the parent species.

8. Sympatric species are closely related species whose distribution overlaps. Allopatric species are species that remain geographically separated.

143. Sympatric Speciation (page 193)

1. **Sympatric speciation**: A speciation event that occurs without prior geographical separation. The two species are separated by some other means such as niche differentiation, or may be separated by a spontaneous chromosomal change (polyploidy).

2. Polyploidy creates extra chromosome sets for an individual that make it impossible for it to reproduce with members of its parental population. Hybrids may form but they will be sterile.

3. Modern wheat, swedes

4. If two groups within a species population have slightly different habitats and food or foraging preferences (niche differentiation), then they will not come into contact for mating.

144. Stages in Species Development (page 194)

1. Some butterflies rested on top of boulders, others rested in the grass.

2. Selection pressure on BSBs is the need to maintain operating body temperature at the high altitude (fitness is higher when

© 2015 **BIOZONE** International
ISBN:978-1-927309-27-8
Photocopying Prohibited

they can efficiently absorb heat from boulders). Selection pressure on the GSBs is probably predation as these lowland butterflies survive better where they avoid detection.

145. The Evolution of Antibiotic Resistance (page 195)

1. Antibiotic resistance refers to the resistance bacteria show to antibiotics that would normally inhibit their growth. In other words, they no longer show a reduction in growth response in the presence of the antibiotic.

2. (a) Antibiotic resistance arises in a bacterial population as result of mutation.
   (b) Resistance can become widespread as a result of (1) transfer of genetic material between bacteria (horizontal gene transfer) or by (2) increasing resistance with each generation a result of natural selection processes (vertical evolution).

3. Methicillin resistant *Staphylococcus aureus* (MRSA) have acquired genes for resistance to penicillin and related antibiotics, so these antibiotics are no longer effective against MRSA. This is a problem because S. aureus infections are very common and they are becoming more difficult to treat and control. If resistance continues to develop, there may be no way of treating them in the future.

146. Antigenic Variability in *Influenzavirus* (page 196)

1. (a) The viral genome is contained on 8 short, loosely connected RNA segments. This enables ready exchange of genes between different viral strains and leads to alteration on the protein composition of the H and N glycoprotein spikes.
   (b) The body's immune system acquires antibodies to the H and N spikes (antigens) on the viral surface, but when different variants arise they are not recognised nor detected by the immune system (there is no immunological memory for the newly appearing antigens).

2. An antigenic shift represents the combination of two or more different viral strains in a new subtype with new properties and no immunological history in the population. Antigenic drifts are much smaller changes that occur continually over time and to which small adjustments are sufficient to provide resistance.

147. Resistance in HIV (page 197)

1. Drug resistance arises as a result of mutations in the viral genome that alter drug binding or otherwise increase viral fitness. When resistance arises, resistant variants will proliferate. HIV's mutation rate is rapid, so resistance is continually arising.

2. HIV mutates quickly and so has a very high genetic diversity, even in one individual. A vaccine primes the immune system to target specific viral properties (e.g. surface proteins) but frequent mutations mean those properties keep changing. A vaccine will only work for as long as the viral properties remain unchanged.

3. HIV's high genetic diversity and rapid mutation rate mean that a variety of drugs targeting different parts of the HIV life cycle will be most effective. There will then be a lower chance that viral strains will be resistant to all the drugs.

148. Chloroquine Resistance in Protozoa (page 198)

1. Chloroquine was very cheap to manufacture, was well tested and safe to administer, and had few side effects. Until resistance developed, it was also very effective at preventing malaria infection.

2. Chloroquine resistance in *P. falciparum* is based on the fact that they accumulate significantly less chloroquine than susceptible parasites. The mechanism for this appears to be due to a mutation at amino acid position 76 conferring an enhanced ability to release the chloroquine from the vesicles in which it normally accumulates in the cell.

3. (a) Combination of drug therapies.
   (b) Temporary withdrawal of chloroquine (for short periods) while using other drugs to retain chloroquine efficacy.

149. Biodiversity (page 199)

1. Species diversity refers to the number of different species within an area (species richness), while genetic diversity describes the diversity of genes within a particular species. Biodiversity is defined as the measure of all genes, species, and ecosystems in a region, so both genetic and species diversity are important in evaluating total biodiversity.

2. Different species have different habitat preferences, so within a larger heterogeneous region, a variety of different habitats can potentially can support a greater species diversity.

3. (a) Species richness measures the number of species within an ecosystem, whereas species evenness describes how equally the species are distributed within an ecosystem.
   (b) Both measures are important when considering species conservation. Species richness could give an indication of ecosystem stability, and therefore how at-risk particular species may be. Species evenness provides an indication of the species distribution (a limited distribution or a distribution where individuals are widely separated may indicate the species is at risk).

4. Keystone species are pivotal to some important ecosystem function such as production of biomass or nutrient recycling. Because their role is disproportionately large, their removal has a similarly disproportionate effect on ecosystem function.

5. **Grey wolf**: Wolves, as a top predator, are an integral component of the ecosystems to which they belong. The wide range of habitats in which they thrive reflects their adaptability as a species. Their diet includes elk, caribou, moose, deer and other large ungulates, as well as smaller prey. Wolves are sensitive to fluctuations in prey abundance, and the balance between wolves and their prey preserves the ecological balance between large herbivores and available forage.

   European beaver: When beavers build dams, innumerable species, many of which may be threatened or endangered, benefit. As well as creating habitat, beaver ponds encourage the growth of aquatic vegetation and also result in increases in invertebrate populations. This in turn provides an enhanced food source for fish, amphibians and birds, which also benefits predators higher up the food chain (e.g. otters, grey herons) which eat the fish. Beavers are entirely herbivorous and their activity is closely tied to the regeneration of deciduous woodland tree species, including aspen, birch, oak, and rowan. Beavers eat the bark of these trees and, by harvesting the trees, promote regeneration and stand replacement.

   Scots pine: The Scots pine has relationships with many organisms. Some are associated directly with the pine itself, particularly epiphytic lichens, mosses, and mycorrhizal fungi, including the chanterelle and the extremely rare greenfoot tooth fungus. Scots pine provides habitat for a number of plant species with restricted distribution, including blaeberries and cowberries, which play a successional role in the development of the hummocks characteristic of the Scots pinewood ecosystems. A wide variety of invertebrate, mammal, and bird species, some of which are endemic and/or endangered, are also dependent directly or indirectly on the Scots pine (e.g. for habitat or food).

150. Sampling Populations (page 201)

1. We sample populations in order to gain information about their abundance and composition. Sampling is necessary because, in most cases, populations are too large to examine in total.

2. Random sampling removes bias which may influence the result of the study.

3. (a) The population is divided into mutually exclusive groups and therefore effectively separate groups (e.g. male and female). Random sampling can be applied to each group; effectively there are two separate sampling events.
   (b) Stratified sampling often occurs in large scale surveys, e.g political opinion polls, identifying differences in suburban, semi-rural, and rural populations.

4. (a) A student might use the school roll and select every 4th person on the roll, or select every 3rd person in every classroom roll.

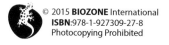

(b) A student might divide the school students into males and females or into year groups, before conducting a random survey.
(c) The student may stop students in the hall between classes or at lunch break to gather information.

151. Interpreting Samples (page 202)

1. (a) The pH decreases
   (b) The increase in plant cover helps maintain moisture at ground level. Loss of organic matter from the plants (e.g. fallen leaves) add to the organic matter (humus). Moisture increases sharply at the wet slack due to the sheltered position between the dunes and the water table being close to the surface.

2. (a) 0.4 m
   (b) Lichens (various species).
   (c) Most mosses need higher moisture and lower light and temperatures than lichens.

152. Assessing Species Diversity (page 203)

1. (a) 7 + 10 + 11 + 2 + 4 + 3 = 37. 37 x 36 = 1332. (7x6) + (10x9) + (11x10) + (2x1) + (4x3) + (3x2) = 262. 1332 / 262 = **5.08**
   (b) 16 + 4 + 1 + 3 + 4 + 2 = 30. 30 x 29 = 870. (16x4) + (4x3) + (1x0) + (3x2) + (4x3) + (2x1) = 272. 870 / 272 = **3.20**
   (c) The forest floor community is more diverse that the one near the forest margin.

153. Investigating Biodiversity (page 204)

1. Systematic

2. (a) An appropriate size of sampling unit enables you to sample the organisms effectively and collect enough data for the samples to be representative of the population(s) involved, without extra, unnecessary data collection.
   (b) Making some reasonable assumptions allows you to focus on the questions that you really want to answer and offer plausible explanations if your results do not support your predictions. It also allows you to recognise the limitations of the investigation.
   (c) Apart from standard moral obligations to do no damage, consideration of the environment is essential to being able to justify any repeat of your work, and to ensure that any repeat takes place in the same system. For the investigation to be relevant it must be carried in a relevant environment using an appropriate sampling technique.
   (d) Organisms should always be returned to the same area to avoid introducing new organisms into regions where they may previously have been absent, and to minimise the impact of sampling on the area being investigated. This is especially important if sampling is to occur on many different occasions (e.g. annually).
   (e) The sample area must cover all the possible locations that the organisms might be as to remove any bias towards a particular habitat. The total area sampled should also be appropriate to the size of the organism(s) being sampled and the questions being asked. Example: In a study of altitudinal zonation, a very short transect in a small area would not be representative of community changes.

2. (a) Site 1

Species	Number of animals	n-1	n(n-1)
1	35	34	1190
2	14	13	182
3	13	12	156
4	12	11	132
5	8	7	56
6	6	5	30
7	6	5	30
8	4	3	12
		Σn(n-1) =	1788

Site 2

Species	Number of animals	n-1	n(n-1)
1	74	73	5402
2	20	19	380
3	3	2	6
4	3	2	6
5	1	0	0
6	0	0	0
7	0	0	0
8	0	0	0
		Σn(n-1) =	5794

(b) 98 x 97 = 9506 / 1788 = 5.31
(c) 100 x 99 = 9900 / 5794 = 1.71
(d) The diversity of the oak wood is greater than that of the pine plantations. This may be because the oak wood is likely to have a greater variety of plant species and that oak leaves decompose more readily than those of conifer trees, providing a greater leaf litter habitat.

154. Assessing Genetic Diversity (page 206)

1. Genetic diversity refers to the variety of alleles and genotypes present within a population.

2. (a) ADA enzyme locus
   (b) 6 / 26 = 0.23

3. (a) Low population numbers meant that there was a high degree of inbreeding. As a result, fertility rates (and production of viable offspring) decreased. This further decreased population numbers, making the inbreeding problem worse.
   (b) The introduced birds increased genetic diversity and increased genetic fitness of the population (more viable offspring were produced, so population numbers increased).

155. Why is Biodiversity Important? (page 207)

1. High diversity ecosystems have a more complex network of species interactions than low diversity systems and this may provide a buffering effect against change, i.e. greater stability.

2. Benefits include:
   – General enjoyment of the environment.
   – Inspiration for artists (and the economic benefits of this).
   – Ecotourism (not really an aesthetic reason, but is a result of the aesthetics of environment).

3. (a) Genetic resources are genes that may have benefit (even if currently not realised) for humans e.g. genes that produce anticancer agents in plants.
   (b) The loss of biodiversity also reduces genetic diversity, which reduces the genetic resources potentially available.

4. The situation could have been prevented by planting a wider variety of potato crops. This would have meant that whereas some crops were destroyed, others may have survived.

5. Economic benefits include products derived from the environment, e.g. food and clean water, medicines and biochemicals, and various fibres. There are also indirect but important regulating services which, if done by human technology would cost billions upon billions of dollars. These include regulation of the climate, disease, water quality and storage, and pollination. There are also economic benefits derived from cultural ideals, including recreation, ecotourism, and education.

156. How Humans Affect Biodiversity (page 209)

1. Student's own answer. Should include discussions on:
   – Increase in human population increases demand for resources.
   – Population increase results in fragmentation of habitats as cities expand.
   – Increase in population increase demand for food and

therefore demand for space to agriculture.

2. (a) The current rate of extinction is much higher than the estimated background rate. In some cases it is as much as 1000 times higher.
   (b) Most of this difference is due directly or indirectly to human activity.

3. (a) Corals
   (b) Amphibians
   (c) The index can help highlight species in danger of extinction and therefore also highlight environments and habitats that need to be protected.

4. Student's own answer based on information from the weblinks.

157. *In-situ* Conservation (page 211)

1. (a) Advantages of *in-situ* conservation include:
   - Species have access to their natural resources, such as their normal range of food and breeding sites.
   - Being in their natural environment will help conserve their natural behaviour.
   - A greater number of species can be protected at one time.
   - The cost is lower than a captive breeding programme

   (b) Difficulties with *in-situ* conservation include:
   - There can be considerable difficulties in protecting *in-situ* populations from exploitation.
   - Habitats often need extensive restoration and then protection before being suitable for *in-situ* conservation. This can be difficult for large areas that may cross state or country boundaries.
   - Declines may be difficult to stop if the population has reached critically low levels.

2. *In situ* conservation uses ecosystem management and legislation to protect species in their natural habitat. By necessity, this involves both restoring the ecosystem and implementing laws to protect the species of interest. Methods include protecting and/or restoring the habitat, and protecting the endangered species from predators, hunting, and illegal trade (e.g. by CITES). Neither tool is effective in isolation; if the species are not protected, there is little point is restoring their habitat and if they are without habitat, there is little point in protecting them.

3. Student's own answer based on their own research.

158. Hedgerows (page 213)

1. (a)-(c) any advantages of:
   - Hedgerows provide habitat and food for wildlife.
   - Hedgerows act as corridors along which animals can move between regions of suitable habitat (e.g. for feeding). Corridors are also important for the establishment and expansion of some plant species.
   - Hedgerows shelter stock and reduce wind speed, thereby reducing erosion.
   - Hedgerows provide habitat for pollinating insects and the predators of pest species. This may benefit the farmer.

2. Hedgerows might be regarded as undesirable because:
   - Hedgerows hamper effective use of some farm machinery.
   - Hedgerows take up space that could otherwise be used for grazing or crop production.
   - Hedgerows provide habitat for competitors to grazing livestock (e.g. hares) and predators (foxes).

3. Retaining well managed hedgerows offers the farmer many benefits. Hedges provide shelter for stock and reduce wind speeds, which stops erosion. Hedges provide habitat for helpful bird and insect species, which can prey on harmful pest insects and prevent spikes in pest populations. The also prevent the spread of wind-borne insect pests. Well managed hedges are also and eco-friendly cost-effective alternative to other types of fencing.

159. *Ex-situ* Conservation (page 214)

1. *Ex-situ* conservation methods are often employed when species numbers become critically low or *in-situ* methods are not working. Features of *ex-situ* conservation focus on (1)

removal of the endangered species from its natural habitat to a new location, usually a protected or controlled area and (2) captive breeding (or cultivation) involving a managed breeding (seed) register to maximise remaining genetic diversity.

2. Not all animal species adapt well to captivity. Some species will not breed successfully in captivity or have very specific social requirements that might not be met by the conditions. Conversely, those individuals (and species) that adapt most successfully to breeding in captivity are inadvertently selected for survival in zoos, therefore their return to the wild might be compromised.

3. (a) Public education to promote species conservation and increase awareness.
   (b) To participate in global breeding programmes to secure the viability of threatened species.
   (c) Zoos act as custodians for rare species; they cannot save a species from extinction if breeding is unsuccessful, but they can protect breeding individuals while other plans are implemented.

4. Gene banks and seedbanks provide a store of genetic diversity from wild stocks so that the genetic diversity is preserved in the advent of species loss or decline. Using modern reproductive technologies, gene banks can be used to boost the genetic diversity of inbred populations of endangered species. They also house genetic diversity from which to improve food crops and domestic livestock breeds. Wild species have characteristics (e.g. disease resistance, hardiness) that could be useful in agricultural production and it is important that this store of diversity is not lost.

5. *In situ* conservation involves a whole-ecosystem management approach to saving species in their own natural environment. Methods include protecting or restoring the habitat, and protecting endangered species from losses (e.g. from introduced predators, illegal trade, and hunting). If whole-ecosystem restoration is successful, it offers a good chance of species recovery, even for critically endangered species. It has the advantages of less disturbance to the species involved, it by-passes the need for captive breeding (which is unsuccessful for some species), and it offers a greater chance of long term success because habitat restoration goes hand in hand with species management. *Ex-situ* conservation methods are often used when species numbers become critically low or *in-situ* methods are not working or are not feasible. *Ex-situ* conservation involves removing the endangered species from its natural habitat to a new location, where it can be monitored and protected more easily. *Ex-situ* methods rarely save species from extinction, and are often costly and labour intensive. Because the breeding stock is also limited, genetic diversity of the species may also become compromised.

160. Chapter Review (page 216)

No model answer. Summary is the student's own.

161. KEY TERMS: Mix and Match (page 218)

1. adaptation (F), allopatric speciation (C), biodiversity (D), bioinformatics (E), binomial nomenclature (B), conservation (J), diversity indices (A), domain (P), *ex-situ* conservation (G), fitness (I), *in-situ* conservation (O), natural selection (N), phylogeny (H), reproductive isolation (K), species (M), sympatric speciation (L)

2. A: High species evenness but with a low species richness.
   B: Low species evenness but high species richness.

162. The Structure of Membranes (page 221)

1. (a) Channel and carrier proteins
   (b) Carrier proteins
   (c) Glycoproteins, glycolipids
   (d) Cholesterol

2. Phospholipids have hydrophilic heads and hydrophobic tails. The molecules orientate so that the hydrophilic head is towards the exterior of the membrane and the hydrophobic tail is towards the interior. This forms the a lipid bilayer and the

© 2015 **BIOZONE** International
ISBN:978-1-927309-27-8
Photocopying Prohibited

basis of the plasma membrane.

3. (a) Membranes are composed of a phospholipid bilayer in which are embedded proteins, glycoproteins, and glycolipids. The structure is relatively fluid and the proteins are able to move within this fluid matrix.
   (b) This model accounts for the properties we observe in cellular membranes: its fluidity (how its shape is not static and how its components move within the membrane, relative to one-another) and its mosaic nature (the way in which the relative proportions of the membrane components, i.e. proteins, glycoproteins, glycolipids etc, can vary from membrane to membrane). The fluid mosaic model also accounts for how membranes can allow for the selective passage of materials (e.g. through protein channels) and how they enable cell-cell recognition (a result of membrane components such as glycoproteins).

4. (a) Enable the passage of specific molecules into the cell by facilitated diffusion or active transport.
   (b) Provide a hydrophilic pore through the membrane so that water soluble molecules pass easily through.

5. (a) Non-polar molecules can dissolve in the lipid bilayer structure of the membrane and diffuse into the cell whereas the polar molecules must be actively transported through the membrane
   (b) Diffusion of lipid-soluble molecules across the plasma membrane is rapid (increasing efficiency of substrate delivery) and saves energy (transport is passive).

6. Cholesterol lies between the phospholipids and maintains membrane integrity and fluidity (preventing crystallisation).

7. (a)-(c) in any order: oxygen, food (glucose), minerals and trace elements, water.

8. (a) Carbon dioxide   (b) Nitrogenous wastes

9. Plasma membrane:

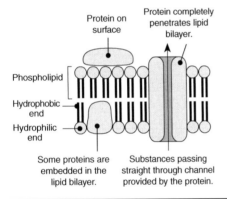

163. How Do We Know? Membrane Structure
   (page 223)
1. The impressions left in one side of the membrane after freeze fracture give evidence of proteins located within the membrane. Fracturing the membrane allowed scientists to observe the presence of integral membrane proteins which span the membrane lipid bilayer. This supported the fluid mosaic model, in which membrane-bound proteins are able to move relatively freely within the membrane.

2. If the bilayer had a continuous protein coat, the freeze fracture specimen would look flat and uniform when viewed under the electron microscope. The proteins are discrete complexes randomly spaced throughout the lipid bilayer. The bumps observed indicates where the proteins were located.

164. Factors Altering Membrane Permeability
   (page 224)
1. Washing the beetroot in distilled water removes any pigment that might be present due to leaching as a result of cutting.

2 (a)

Temperature °C	Mean
0	0.0055
20	0.223
40	0.108
60	0.538
90	3

   (b) As temperature increases, membrane permeability also increases.
   (c) It occurs because there is increasing damage to the tonoplast as temperature is increased.

3. The 0% ethanol solution acts as a control for comparison to the other concentrations.

4 (a) The parafilm stops the ethanol from evaporating.
   (b) The evaporated ethanol when cause a change in concentration of the ethanol/water solution. The results would not be accurate.

5. (a)

Ethanol concentration/ %	Mean
0	0.030
6.25	0.016
12.5	0.023
25	0.082
50	0.925
100	1.184

   (b)

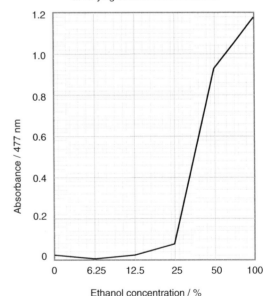

Absorbance of beetroot samples at varying ethanol concentrations.

   (c) As ethanol concentration increases, membrane permeability also increases.

6. Ethanol causes proteins in the membrane to be denatured. This causes the membrane to lose its selective permeability and become leakier.

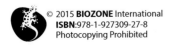

165. Diffusion (page 226)

1. Diffusion is the passive movement of particles down a concentration gradient (from high to low concentration).

2. They involve movement of substances across a membrane with no input of energy (they are passive).

3. Facilitated diffusion involves channels, which allow ions to pass through the membrane. Ions are charged, so they cannot simply diffuse across the nonpolar interior of the lipid bilayer.

166. Osmosis (page 227)

1. Osmosis is the diffusion of water molecules across a partially permeable membrane from a region of lower solute concentration (higher free water molecule concentration) to a region of higher solute concentration (lower free water molecule concentration).

2. (a) The net movement of water is from right to left:

   (b) The water moved into the dialysis tubing because it contained the sucrose solution, and therefore had a higher solute concentration and a lower concentration of free water molecules. The water moved down its concentration gradient.

3. The height of the water would increase.

167. Water Movement in Plant Cells (page 228)

1. Zero

2. (a) -100 → -200 water moves to cell on the right
   (b) -400 ↔ -400 no net movement
   (c) -400 ← -200 water moves to the cell on the left

3. Dissolved solutes lower the water potential (make it more negative).

4. The plasma membrane pushes up against the cell wall which is rigid and stops the cell from bursting.

5. (a) Plasmolysis is the pulling away of the plasma membrane from the cell wall, caused by a lack of water in the cell. Turgor is the pressing of the cell membrane against the cell wall as a result of water entering the cell.
   (b) The plant has wilted due to a lack of water. The cells in the plant have plasmolysed and lost their rigidity causing the plant to collapse.

6. (a) Pressure potential generated within plant cells provides the turgor to support unlignified plant tissues.
   (b) Without cell turgor, soft plant tissues (soft stems and flower parts for example) would lose support and wilt. Note that some tissues are supported by structural components such as lignin.

168. Making Dilutions (page 230)

1. (a) 3.75 cm³ stock solution needed
   (b) 2.5 cm³ stock solution needed
   (c) 1.25 cm³ stock solution needed

2. (a) 0.75 mol dm⁻³ = -1838.59 kPa
       0.50 mol dm⁻³ = -1225.73 kPa
       0.25 mol dm⁻³ = -612.86 kPa
       1.00 mol dm⁻³ = -2451.45 kPa
   (b)

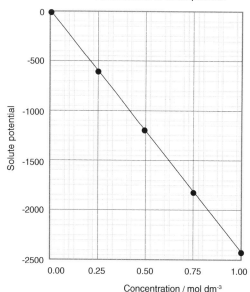

169. Estimating Osmolarity (page 231)

1.

   Completed table (totals section only)

0.00 Mol dm⁻³		Initial mass (g)	Final mass (g)
Total		15.46	17.22
Change (g)	1.76		
% Change	11.38%		
0.25 Mol dm⁻³		Initial mass (g)	Final mass (g)
Total		19.18	17.93
Change (g)	-1.25		
% Change	-6.52%		
0.50 Mol dm⁻³		Initial mass (g)	Final mass (g)
Total		18.26	16.14
Change (g)	-2.12		
% Change	-11.61%		
0.75 Mol dm⁻³		Initial mass (g)	Final mass (g)
Total		19.16	13.99
Change (g)	-5.17		
% Change	-26.98%		
1.00 Mol dm⁻³		Initial mass (g)	Final mass (g)
Total		16.14	13.00
Change (g)	-3.14		
% Change	-19.45%		

2.

Concentration vs % Change

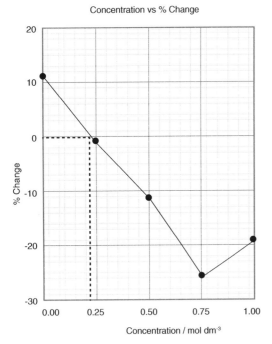

3. (a) Approximately 0.23 mol dm^{-3}
   (b) -563.8 kPa
   (c) 0 kPa
   (d) -563.8 kPa

---

170. Diffusion and Cell Size (page 232)

1.
Cube	Surface area	Volume	Ratio
3 cm:	3 x 3 x 6 = 54	3 x 3 x 3 = 27	2.0 to 1
4 cm:	4 x 4 x 6 = 96	4 x 4 x 4 = 64	1.5 to 1
5 cm:	5 x 5 x 6 = 150	5 x 5 x 5 = 125	1.2 to 1

2. Surface area to volume graph:

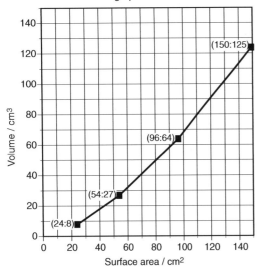

3. Volume

4. Increasing size leads to less surface area for a given volume. The surface area to volume ratio decreases.

5. (a)
Cube	1	2	3
Total volume	1	8	64
Volume not pink	0.125 (0.5^3)	3.375 (1.5^3)	42.8 (3.5^3)
Diffused volume	0.875	4.625	21.2
Percentage diffusion	87.5	57.8	33.1

(b) An increase in cell size reduces the ability of diffusion to transport molecules into and out of a cell at the rate required to maintain the cell's original metabolic rate. (i.e. volume increases faster that surface area and thus the proportion of molecules diffusing across the plasma membrane decreases in relation to the size of the cell).

6. A cell measuring 1 cm x 1 cm x 1 cm has a surface area of 6 cm^3. Eight of them will have a volume of 8 cm^3 but a surface area of 42 cm^2. A cell measuring 2 cm x 2 cm x 2 cm will have a volume of 8 cm^3 but a surface area of only 24 cm^2. Thus eight small cells are more able to acquire nutrients due to their larger surface area to volume ratios.

---

171. Active Transport (page 234)

1. Active transport is the energy using process of moving molecules or ions against their concentration gradient.

2. ATP.

3. Primary active transport uses energy gained directly from ATP. Secondary active transport uses energy in the form of a concentration gradient formed by transport proteins using ATP for energy.

---

172. Ion Pumps (page 235)

1. ATP (directly or indirectly) supplies the energy to move substances against their concentration gradient.

2. (a) Cotransport describes coupling the movement of a molecule (such as sucrose or glucose) against its concentration gradient to the diffusion of an ion (e.g. H$^+$ or Na$^+$) down its concentration gradient. Note: An energy requiring ion exchange pump is used to establish this concentration gradient.
   (b) In the gut, a gradient in sodium ions is used to drive the transport of glucose across the epithelium. A Na$^+$/K$^+$ pump (requiring ATP) establishes an unequal concentration of Na$^+$ across the membrane. A specific membrane protein then couples the return of Na$^+$ down its concentration gradient to the transport of glucose.
   (c) The glucose diffuses from the epithelial cells of the gut into the blood, where it is transported away. This maintains a low level in the intestinal epithelial cells.

3. Extracellular accumulation of Na$^+$ (any two of):
   – maintains the gradient that is used to cotransport useful molecules, such as glucose, into cells.
   – maintains cell volume by creating an osmotic gradient that drives the absorption of water
   – establishes and maintains resting potential in nerve and muscle cells
   – provides the driving force for several facilitated membrane transport proteins.

---

173. Excocytosis and Endocytosis (page 236)

1. Phagocytosis is the engulfment of solid material by endocytosis whereas pinocytosis is the uptake of liquids or fine suspensions by endocytosis.

2. Phagocytosis examples (any of):
   • Feeding in *Amoeba* by engulfing material using cytoplasmic extensions called pseudopodia.
   • Ingestion of old red blood cells by Küpffer cells in the liver.
   • Ingestion of bacteria and cell debris by phagocytic white blood cells.

3. Exocytosis examples:
   - Secretion of substances from specialised secretory cells in multicellular organisms, e.g. hormones from endocrine cells, digestive secretions from exocrine cells.
   - Expulsion of wastes from unicellular organisms, e.g. *Paramecium* and *Amoeba* expelling residues from food vacuoles.

4. (a) Oxygen: Diffusion.
   (b) Cellular debris: Phagocytosis.
   (c) Water: Osmosis.
   (d) Glucose: Facilitated diffusion.

174. Active and Passive Transport Summary (page 237)
1. A. Diffusion
   B. Osmosis
   C. Facilitated diffusion
   D. Ion pump (or sodium-potassium pump)
   E. Pinocytosis
   F. Exocytosis
   G. Phagocytosis

2. Passive transport requires no energy input from the cell (materials move down a concentration gradient). Active transport requires energy (ATP) to move substances against their concentration gradient.

3. Gases moving by diffusion: Oxygen, carbon dioxide.

4. (a) Pinocytosis
   (b) Phagocytosis.
   (c) Osmosis
   (d) Exocytosis
   (e) Endocytosis
   (f) Phagocytosis
   (g) Facilitated diffusion
   (h) Carrier-mediated facilitated diffusion
   (i) Sodium-potassium pump

175. ATP Supplies Energy for Work (page 238)
1. ATP production occurs in the mitochondrion.

2. ATP hydrolase

3. ATP synthase

4. (a) and (b)

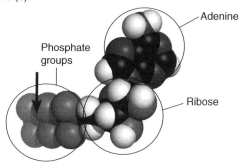

Phosphate groups

Adenine

Ribose

5. Like a rechargeable battery, the ADP/ATP system alternates between a high energy and a low energy state. The addition of a phosphate to ADP recharges the molecule so that it can be used for cellular work.

176. Introduction to Gas Exchange (page 239)
1. Cellular respiration refers to production of ATP via oxidation of glucose. Gas exchange refers to the way in which respiratory gases are exchanged with the environment. Oxygen is required to drive the reactions of cellular respiration. CO_2 is a waste product.

2. (a) Oxygen and CO_2 (b) Diffusion.

3. A gas exchange surface provides a surface across which gases can diffuse.

4. (a) Associated with mechanisms (e.g. blood flow) to maintain the concentration gradient.

(b) Large surface area to provide for high rates of gas exchange (enough to meet the organism's needs).
(c) Thin membrane that does not present a large barrier to diffusion of gases.

5. Root hairs increase the surface area for absorption of water and minerals.

6 (a) Rate of diffusion increases
   (b) Rate of diffusion increases
   (c) Rate of diffusion decreases

7. Mammals maintain an oxygen gradient by constantly moving air into and out of the lungs by breathing. Fresh air is breathed in (inspiration), oxygen moves into the blood, and oxygen-deficient air is expelled (expiration).

177. Gas Exchange in Animals (page 241)
1. (a) Provides adequate supply and removal of respiratory gases necessary for an active lifestyle.
   (b) Enables animals to attain a larger size (as they are freed from a dependence on direct diffusion of gases across thin body surfaces).

2. (a) Air breathers produce mucus that keeps the gas exchange surface moist.
   (b) Some water vapour is present in lungs as a result of metabolism.

3. Gills are external structures and need support from a dense medium (water). In air, they would collapse.

4. Breathing keeps air moving and maintains the concentration gradient for the diffusion of gases (CO_2 out and O_2 in).

178. The Human Gas Exchange System (page 242)
1. (a) The structural arrangement (lobes, each with its own bronchus and dividing many times before terminating in numerous alveoli) provides an immense surface area for gas exchange.
   (b) Gas exchange takes place in the alveoli.

2. The alveolar-capillary membrane is the layered junction between the alveolar cells, the endothelial cells of the capillaries, and their associated basement membranes. It provides a surface across which gases can move freely by diffusion.

3. Surfactant reduces the surface tension of the lung tissue and counteracts the tendency of the alveoli to recoil inward and stick together after each expiration.

4. Completed table as below:

Region	Cartilage	Ciliated epithelium	Goblet cells (mucus)	Smooth muscle	Connective tissue
❶ Trachea	✓	✓	✓	✓	✓
❷ Bronchus	✓	✓	✓	✓	✓
❸ Bronchioles	gradually lost	✓	✓	✓	✓
❹ Alveolar duct	✗	✗	✗	✓	✓
❺ Alveoli	✗	✗	✗	very little	✓

5. Lack of surfactant results in high surface tension in the alveoli causing them to collapse to an uninflated state after each breath. Breathing is difficult and laboured, and oxygen delivery is inadequate. Untreated, death usually follows in a few hours.

179. Breathing in Humans (page 244)
1. Breathing ventilates the lungs, renewing the supply of fresh (high oxygen) air while expelling air high in CO_2 (gained as a result of gas exchanges in the tissues).

2. Breathing is the result of muscle contraction and relaxation that increases and decreases the volume of the thoracic cavity. The pressure changes that accompany the volume changes cause air to move in and out of the lungs.

 © 2015 BIOZONE International
ISBN:978-1-927309-27-8
Photocopying Prohibited

3. (a) Quiet breathing: External intercostal muscles and diaphragm contract. Lung volume increases and air flows into the lungs (inspiration). Expiration occurs through elastic recoil of the ribcage and lung tissue (air flows passively out to equalise with outside air pressure).
    (b) In active breathing, muscular contraction is involved in both inspiration and expiration (expiration is not passive).

4. (a) External intercostals and diaphragm.
    (b) Internal intercostals and abdominal muscles

5. (a) Internal intercostals and abdominal muscles
    (b) External intercostals and diaphragm.

6. Antagonistic muscles bring about the changes in thoracic volume that enable air to be moved in and out of the lungs. The muscles for inspiration are in opposition to those for expiration. When one set is contracting, the other is relaxed.

180. Investigating Ventilation in Humans (page 245)
1. (a) 3.15 dm^3
    (b) 3.75 dm^3
    (c) Results are as expected.
        Males are generally physically larger than females, so their lung capacities are also larger.

2. (a) and (b)

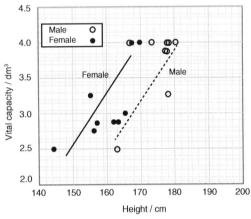

Height vs vital capacity

(c) There is a positive correlation between height and vital capacity.

181. Gas Exchange in Insects (page 246)
1. In insect tracheae, gases move by diffusion directly into the tissues. Gases diffuse into and out of the fluid at the end of the tracheole, and the fluid acts as the medium for gas exchange into the tissues.

2. Valves present in the spiracles control the rate of entry and exit of air into and out of the tracheal system. This enables the rate of gas exchange to be regulated according to the changing activity levels (and therefore gas exchange requirements) of the insect.

3. Ventilation occurs when the insect makes rhythmic body movements helping to move the air in and out of the tracheae.

4. Tracheal systems provide direct delivery of oxygen to the tissues. This system is rapid and efficient for small sized organisms and reduces reliance on water (water is a necessity for organisms relying on diffusion across a moist body surface). A reduced dependence on freely available water has allowed insects to colonise some of the driest places on Earth.

182. Dissection of an Insect (page 247)
1. The spiracles are the openings for the gas exchange system in insects. They can help regulate the amount of air enter the system by opening or closing.

2. (a) Tracheoles end in blind endings within the insect's tissues.
    (b) The air flow is back and forth (by diffusion) through the same tracheal system.

183. Gas Exchange in Fish (page 248)
1. (a)-(c) any of, in any order:
    – Greatly folded surface of gills (high surface area).
    – Gills supported and kept apart from each other by the gas exchange medium (water).
    – Water flow across the gill surface is opposite to that of the blood flow in the gill capillaries (countercurrent), facilitating oxygen uptake.
    – Pumping mechanism of operculum aids movement of the water across the gas exchange surface.

2. Ventilation (moving water across the gill surface) prevents stagnation of the water at the gill surface and maintains the concentration gradient necessary for continued gas exchange.

3. (a) **Pumping**: Operculum acts as a pump, drawing water past the gill filaments.
    (b) **Continuous swimming**: Continuous (usually rapid) swimming with the mouth open produces a constant flow of water over the gill filaments.

4. In countercurrent flow, oxygen-rich water flows over the gill filaments in the opposite direction to the blood flow through the gill filaments. Blood in the capillaries always encounters water with a higher oxygen concentration so the concentration gradient for diffusion into the blood is maintained across the entire gill.

5. (a) As blood flows through the gill capillaries (gaining oxygen) it encounters blood of increasing oxygen content, so a diffusion gradient is maintained across the entire gill surface.
    (b) In parallel flow, the oxygen concentration in the blood and the water would quickly equalise and diffusion into the blood would stop.

6. Oxygen availability in water is low anyway, so anything that lowers this still further (high temperature of decomposition of organic material) increases the vulnerability of fish to oxygen deprivation. This is especially so for fish with high oxygen requirements such as trout and salmon.

184. Gas Exchange in Plants (page 250)
1. (a) and (b) Any two of:
    – Thin blade to maximise the surface area for light capture and gas exchanges.
    – Loosely packed mesophyll facilitates gas movements into and out of the leaf.
    – Transparent so there is no impairment to light entry.
    – Waterproof cuticle reduces transpirational water losses.

2. (a) Net gas exchange (no photosynthesis): net use of oxygen and net production of carbon dioxide.
    (b) Net gas exchange (photosynthesis): net use of carbon dioxide and net production of oxygen.

3. (a) Facilitate diffusion of gases into and out of the leaf.
    (b) Provide a large surface area for gas exchanges (around the cell).

4. Stomata regulate the entry and exit of gases into and out of the leaf (they also regulate water loss).

5. (a) Stomatal opening: Active transport of potassium ions into the guard cells (which lowers the water potential of the guard cells) is followed by osmotic influx of water. This causes the guard cells to swell and become turgid. The structure of the guard cell walls causes them to buckle out, opening the stoma.
    (b) Stomatal closure: Potassium ions leave the guard cell (making the water potential of the guard cells less negative) and water follows by osmosis. The guard cells become flaccid and sag together closing the stoma.

185. Transport in Multicellular Organisms (page 252)
1. As body mass increases the surface area to volume ratio decreases. As this occurs diffusion becomes too inefficient and slow to provide raw materials quickly enough to all the cells of larger animals. Mass transport systems are required to transport materials to and from where they are needed.

2. (a) In vertebrates mass transport is used to transport materials around the body.
   (b) Mass transport systems allow materials to be moved over a long distance in complex multicellular organisms. In contrast, small organisms such as the flatworm or single celled eukaryotes have a surface area to volume ratio large enough to allow for materials to be efficiently transported by diffusion.
   (c) The tissues and either the gills or lungs.

186. Closed Circulatory Systems (page 253)

1. Unlike closed systems, open circulatory systems do not have a complete circuit of vessels for blood to pass through from the heart to the body and back again.

2. (a) Blood passes from the gills to the body.
   (b) Blood flows through the systemic circulation at low pressure.

3. (a) Blood returns to the heart after the lungs.
   (b) Blood flows through the systemic circulation at higher pressure than in the single circuit system.

4. By passing blood back to the heart from the lungs, the double circuit system is able to maintain high blood pressure throughout the body. Higher systemic pressures are important for efficient oxygen delivery and processes like renal filtration (which is less important in fish, which use the gills for excretion).

5. (a) The fish heart is a single pump. Blood flows from the atrium to the ventricle and on to the general circulation.
   (b) The mammalian heart is a double pump with two atria and two ventricles separated by a muscular septum. One pump sends blood to the lungs, the other sends blood to the body.

6. Blood flow within vessels can be regulated by the contraction or relaxing of blood vessel walls. This enables animals to restrict blood flow in some areas and increase it in others in response to need.

187. The Mammalian Transport System (page 255)

1. (a) Head   (d) Gut (intestines)
   (b) Lungs   (e) Kidneys
   (c) Liver   (f) Genitals/lower body

2. Circle pulmonary artery and pulmonary vein.

188. Arteries (page 256)

1. (a) Tunica externa   (c) Endothelium
   (b) Tunica media   (d) Blood (or lumen)

2. Thick, elastic walls are required in order to withstand and maintain the high pressure of the blood being pumped from the heart. The elasticity also helps to even out the surges occurring with each heart beat.

3. The smooth muscle around arteries helps to regulate blood flow and pressure. By contracting or relaxing it alters the diameter of the artery and adjusts the volume of blood as required.

4. Arteries have layers of muscle and elastic tissue, which enables them to expand (vasodilation) or constrict (vasoconstriction) to regulate the blood pressure by increasing or decreasing the diameter of the artery lumen

189. Veins (page 257)

1. (a) Veins have less elastic and muscle tissue than arteries.
   (b) Veins have a larger lumen than arteries.

2. Blood in arteries travels at high pressure, so arteries are thick, strong and stretchy, with a lot of elastic tissue to resist and maintain the pressure. Blood in veins travels at lower pressure so veins do not need to be as strong. They have thinner layers of muscle and elastic tissue and a relatively larger lumen.

3. Valves (with muscular movements) help to return venous blood to the heart by preventing backflow away from the heart.

4. Venous blood oozes out in an even flow from a wound

because it has lost a lot of pressure after passing through the narrow capillary vessels (with their high resistance to flow). Arterial blood spurts out rapidly because it is being pumped directly from the heart and has not yet entered the capillaries.

190. Capillaries (page 258)

1. Capillaries exchange oxygen and nutrients in the blood with carbon dioxide and wastes from the cells.

2. Capillaries are very small blood vessels forming networks that penetrate all parts of the body. The only tissue present is an endothelium of squamous epithelial cells. In contrast, arteries have a thin endothelium, a central layer of elastic tissue and smooth muscle and an outer layer of elastic and connective tissue that anchors the vessel. Veins have a thin endothelium, a central layer of elastic and muscle tissue and a relatively thick outer layer of connective tissue. Veins also have valves.

3. Blood contains a large number of all different blood cell types including erythrocytes, leucocytes, and platelets. It also has high levels of glucose, amino acids, and oxygen compared to tissue fluid and lymph. Tissue fluid contains far fewer cells than blood (only leucocytes), no glucose, low levels of amino acids and oxygen, and higher levels of carbon dioxide (produced by the cells of the tissues). Lymph is similar in composition to tissue fluid, but has more lymphocytes (a type of leucocyte). Blood and tissue fluid both contain proteins and hormones but these are absent from lymph.

191. Capillary Networks (page 259)

1. Capillaries are branching networks of fine blood vessels where exchanges between blood and tissue take place. Blood enters the network at the arteriolar end and is collected by venules at the venous end. The true capillaries form a vast network outside of the vascular shunt.

2. The smooth muscle sphincters regulate the blood flow to the capillary network by contracting to restrict blood flow to the network and relaxing to allow blood to flow in. The vascular shunt connects the arteriole and venule and allows blood to bypass the capillaries when the smooth muscle sphincters are contracted.

3. (a) Situation A would occur when the body is restricting blood flow to the capillaries, for example when trying to conserve heat by diverting blood away from the extremities.
   (b) Situation B would occur when the body is trying to remove excess heat by diverting blood to the skin and extremities or when the body is trying to provide extra blood to areas of high metabolism, e.g. when exercising or digesting food.

4. A portal venous system drains blood from one capillary network into another. An example is the hepatic portal system which drains blood from the capillary network in the gut lumen to the capillary network in the liver. Normally capillary networks drain into veins that return directly to the heart.

192. The Role and Formation of Tissue Fluid (page 260)

1. The tissue fluid bathes the tissues, providing oxygen and nutrients as well as a medium for the transport (away) of metabolic wastes, e.g. CO_2.

2. Capillaries are very small blood vessels forming networks or beds that penetrate all parts of the body. Capillary walls are thin enough to allow gas exchange between the capillaries and surrounding tissue.

3. (a) Arteriolar end: Hydrostatic pressure predominates, causing water and solutes to move out of the capillaries.
   (b) Venous end: Reduction in hydrostatic pressure and the retention of proteins within the capillary tends to draw fluid back into the capillary (presence of proteins lowers the solute potential and creates an oncotic pressure, which predominates when hydrostatic pressure falls).

4. (a) Most tissue fluid finds its way directly back into the capillaries as a result of net inward pressure at the venule end of the capillary bed.
   (b) The lymph vessels (which parallel the blood system) drain tissue fluid (as lymph) back into the heart, thereby

© 2015 **BIOZONE** International
ISBN:978-1-927309-27-8
Photocopying Prohibited

returning it into the main circulation.

193. The Human Heart (page 261)
1. (a) Pulmonary artery   (e) Aorta
   (b) Vena cava   (f) Pulmonary vein
   (c) Right atrium (RA)   (g) Left atrium (LA)
   (d) Right ventricle (RV)   (h) Left ventricle (LV)

   Tricuspid valve between RA and RV, bicuspid valve between LA and LV. The semi-lunar valves lie between LV and aorta and between RV and pulmonary artery.

2. Valves prevent the blood flowing the wrong way through the heart and help regulate filling of the chambers.

3. (a) The heart has its own coronary blood supply to meet the high oxygen demands of the heart tissue.
   (b) There must be a system within the heart muscle itself to return deoxygenated blood and waste products of metabolism back to the right atrium.

4. If blood flow to a particular part of the heart is restricted or blocked, the part of the heart muscle supplied by that vessel will die, leading to a heart attack or infarction.

5. A: arterioles   B: venules
   C: arterioles   D: capillaries

6. (a) The pressure in the pulmonary circuit must,be low to prevent accumulation of fluid in the alveoli of the lungs. The systemic circuit must operate at a higher pressure in order to maintain high glomerular (kidney) filtration rates and still have 'enough' pressure to supply blood to the brain.
   (b) The left ventricle must be thicker (than the right) because it pumps blood to the systemic circuit and must develop the higher pressure required by this system. The right side of the heart has a thinner walled ventricle as it must provide a lower pressure pulmonary blood flow.

7. You are recording expansion and recoil of the artery that occurs with each contraction of the left ventricle.

194. Dissecting a Mammalian Heart (page 263)
1.

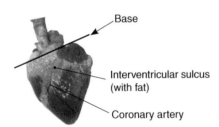

Base

Interventricular sulcus (with fat)

Coronary artery

2. Vena cava

3. Aorta

4. Pulmonary artery

5. Chordae tendineae hold the valves between the atrium and ventricle closed during contraction of the ventricle.

6. The thickness of the ventricle walls (the right ventricle wall is relatively thin while the left ventricle wall is much thicker and very muscular).

195. The Cardiac Cycle (page 265)
1. (a) Aortic pressure is highest when the ventricle is contracting (ventricular pressure also maximum)
   (b) QRS wave immediately precedes increase in ventricular pressure.
   (c) The left ventricle is relaxed and filling.

2. During the period of electrical recovery the heart muscle cannot contract. This ensures that the heart has an enforced rest and will not fatigue, nor accumulate lactic acid (as occurs in working skeletal muscle).

3. Extra text removed and letters placed for each cycle.

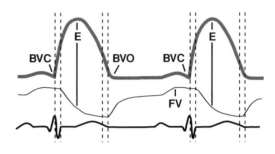

196. Control of Heart Activity (page 266)
1. (a) Sinoatrial node: Initiates the cardiac cycle through the spontaneous generation of action potentials.
   (b) Atrioventricular node: Delays the impulse.
   (c) Bundle of His: Distributes the action potentials over the ventricles (resulting in ventricular contraction).
   (d) Intercalated discs: Electrical junctions that allow the impulses to spread very rapidly through the heart muscle.

2. Delaying the impulse at the AVN allows time for atrial contraction to finish before the ventricles contract.

3. It enables the heart to be able to contract more forcibly if an increased blood volume enters the heart (e.g. during exercise).

4. Influencing heart rate via the CNS allows the heart to deliver blood efficiently in response to demand (e.g. exercise, fight or flight).

197. Recording Changes in Heart Rate (page 267)
1. (a) The graph produced is dependent on student's own response to exercise.
   (b) Students should see an increase in both heart rate and breathing rate during the exercise period.

2. (a) After one minute of rest, students should see a decrease in both heart rate and breathing rate. After five minutes both should have decreased even further, and may have returned to pre-exercise levels.
   (b) Once exercise is completed, the body's metabolic rate falls. The demand for energy and oxygen falls, and the heart rate and breathing rate will fall accordingly.

198. Review of the Heart (page 268)
1. (a) Sinoatrial node (SAN or pacemaker)
   (b) Right atrium
   (c) Atrioventricular node
   (d) Tricuspid valve
   (e) Chordae tendinae
   (f) Bundle of His
   (g) Right ventricle
   (h) Aorta
   (i) Pulmonary artery
   (j) Semi-lunar valve
   (k) Left atrium
   (l) Bicuspid valve
   (m) Purkyne fibres
   (n) Left ventricle

2. A = Contraction of the atria.
   B = Contraction of the ventricles.
   C = Relaxation and filling of ventricles.

3 (a)

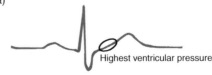

Highest ventricular pressure

(b) Ventricular volume is decreasing

199. Blood (page 269)

1. *Answers given may provide more detail than required.*
   (b) Protection against disease:
   Blood component: White blood cells
   Mode of action: Engulf bacteria, mediate immune reactions, and allergic and inflammatory responses.
   (c) Communication between cells, tissues and organs:
   Blood component: Hormones
   Mode of action: Specific chemicals which are carried in the blood to target tissues, where they interact with specific receptors and bring about an appropriate response.
   (d) Oxygen transport:
   Blood component: Haemoglobin molecule of erythrocytes.
   Mode of action: Binds oxygen at the lungs and releases it at the tissues.
   (e) Carbon dioxide transport:
   Blood components: Mainly plasma (most carbon dioxide is carried as bicarbonate in the plasma, a small amount is dissolved in the plasma). Red blood cells (a small amount (10-20%) of carbon dioxide is carried bound to haemoglobin).
   Mode of action: Diffuses between tissues, plasma, and lungs according to concentration gradient.
   (f) Buffer against pH changes:
   Blood components: Haemoglobin molecule of erythrocytes. Plasma bicarbonate and proteins.
   Mode of action: Free hydrogen ions are picked up and carried by the haemoglobin molecule (removed from solution). Plasma bicarbonate can form either carbonic acid by picking up a hydrogen ion (H^+), or sodium bicarbonate by combining with sodium ions. Negatively charged proteins also associate with H^+.
   (g) Nutrient supply:
   Blood component: Plasma
   Mode of action: Glucose is carried in the plasma and is taken up by cells (made available throughout the body to all tissues).
   (h) Tissue repair:
   Blood components: Platelets and leukocytes
   Mode of action: Platelets initiate the cascade of reactions involved in clotting and wound repair. Leukocytes (some types) engulf bacteria and foreign material, preventing or halting infection.
   (i) Hormone, lipid, and fat soluble vitamin transport:
   Blood component: α-globulins
   Mode of action: α-globulins bind these substances and carry them in the plasma. This prevents them being filtered in the kidneys and lost in the urine.

2. Any of: Presence (WBC) or absence (RBC) of **nucleus**. Colour, reflecting presence (RBC) or absence (WBC) of respiratory pigment, **haemoglobin**. **Shape and size** (smaller, dish shaped RBCs vs larger, rounded WBCs. **Mitochondria** present in WBCs, absent in RBCs.

3. (a) Lack of a nucleus allows more space in the cell to carry Hb (hence greater O_2 carrying capacity).
   (b) Lack of mitochondria forces the red blood cells to metabolise anaerobically so that they do not consume the oxygen they are carrying.

4. (a) Elevated eosinophil count: Allergic response such as hay fever or asthma.
   (b) Elevated neutrophil count: Microbial infection
   (c) Elevated monocyte count: Inflammatory response.
   (d) Elevated lymphocyte count: Infection or response to vaccination.

200. Blood Clotting (page 271)

1. Prevents bleeding and invasion of bacteria. Aids in the maintenance of blood volume.

2. (a) Injury exposes collagen fibres to the blood.
   (b) Chemicals make the surrounding platelets sticky.
   (c) Clumping forms an immediate plug of platelets preventing blood loss.
   (d) Fibrin clot traps red blood cells and reinforces the seal against blood loss.

3. (a) Clotting factors catalyse the conversion of prothrombin to thrombin, the active enzyme that catalyses the production of fibrin.
   (b) If clotting factors were always present, clotting could not be contained; blood would clot when it shouldn't.

201. Atherosclerosis (page 272)

1. Even though a plaque is forming, blood can continue to flow relatively unhindered through blood vessels. It is only when the blood vessel is almost completely closed that symptoms arise. Fit, healthy people may not show any symptoms at all until a plaque ruptures and causes a major blood clot, which can be lethal.

2. – Atherosclerosis is triggered when a vessel is damaged (e.g. by persistent hypertension).
   – LDLs accumulate at the damaged site and macrophages follow forming foam cells.
   – Foam cells accumulate to form an intermediate lesion called a plaque.
   – As the atheroma develops, the smooth muscle cells of the blood vessel die, and scar tissue forms.
   – Calcium salts accumulate forming and a complicated plaque and the arterial wall may ulcerate.
   – The plaque may break away and blood cells may collect at the site of the plaque rupture, causing a blood clot, which may be fatal.

3. People with atherosclerosis are more at risk of suffering an aneurysm, stroke, or heart attack. This is because their blood vessels may become blocked by the plaque itself or by a blood clot formed at the area of damage.

202. Risk Factors for CVD (page 273)

1. (a) Controllable risk factors for CVD are those that can be altered by changing diet or other lifestyle factors, or by controlling a physiological disease state (e.g. high blood pressure, or high blood cholesterol). Uncontrollable risk factors are those over which no control is possible, e.g. genetic predisposition, sex, or age. Note that the impact of uncontrollable factors can be reduced by changing controllable factors.
   (b) Controllable risk factors often occur together because some tend to be causative for others, or at least always associated, e.g. obesity greatly increases the risk of high blood lipids and high blood pressure: all factors increase the risk of CVD.
   (c) Those with several risk factors have a higher chance of developing CVD because the risks are cumulative and add up to present a greater total risk.

2. (a) LDL deposits cholesterol on the endothelial lining of blood vessels, whereas HDL transports cholesterol to the liver where it is processed. A high LDL:HDL ratio is more likely to result in CVD because more cholesterol will be deposited in blood vessels and contribute to atherosclerosis.
   (b) The LDL:HDL ratio is a more accurate predictor of heart disease risk than total cholesterol *per se*, since it more accurately indicates how much cholesterol will be deposited in arteries.

3. (a) The study clearly shows that as body mass index increases there is also an increase in the risk of cardiovascular disease.
   (b) The study's strength is the large number of people included in the study.

203. Reducing the Risk (page 275)

1. As a group, women who exercised (vigorously or walking) three or more times a week had a greatly reduced risk of CHD, relative to those who did not exercise.

2. (a) The relative risk of fatal CHD is less for people consuming more than 5 portions of fruit and vegetables daily.
   (b) ~25% reduction in risk.

3. (a) Deaths from CHD have steadily fallen since 1970. Current levels are approximately 60% less than in 1970 (using percentage decrease formula: (older - newer) ÷ older).
   (b) Rates of smoking in adults have declined over time and are approximately half the level they were in 1970.
   (c) No; a correlation, even a strong one, does not prove direct causation. However, the link can be made on the weight of other supporting evidence.

204. Myoglobin and Haemoglobin (page 276)

1. Myoglobin is monomeric, i.e. made of a single polypeptide chain (it has a tertiary structure). Haemoglobin is tetrameric, i.e. made of four separate chains (it has both a tertiary and a quaternary structure).

2. Myoglobin enables diving animals to store oxygen in the muscles where it will be used during a dive. The more myoglobin there is in the muscles, the more oxygen can be stored.

3. Oxygen is virtually insoluble in water. Haemoglobin increases oxygen solubility by 100 times.

4. (a)

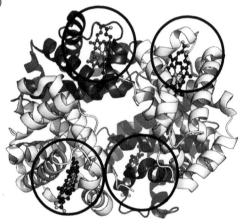

   (b) They are deoxygenated.

5. Fetal haemoglobin contains two γ-chains instead of two β-chains.

205. Gas Transport in Humans (page 277)

1. (a) Oxygen is high in the lung alveoli and in the capillaries leaving the lung.
   (b) Carbon dioxide is high in the capillaries leaving the tissues and in the cells of the body tissues.

2. Haemoglobin binds oxygen reversibly, taking up oxygen when oxygen tensions are high (lungs), carry oxygen to where it is required (the tissues) and release it.

3. (a) As oxygen level in the blood increases, more oxygen combines with haemoglobin. However, the relationship is not linear: Hb saturation remains high even when blood oxygen levels fall very low.
   (b) When oxygen level (partial pressure) in the blood or tissues is low, haemoglobin saturation declines markedly and oxygen is released (to the tissues).

4. (a) Fetal Hb has a higher affinity for oxygen than adult Hb (it can carry 20-30% more oxygen).
   (b) This higher affinity is necessary because it enables oxygen to pass from the maternal Hb to the fetal Hb across the placenta.

5. (a) The Bohr effect.
   (b) Actively respiring tissue consumes a lot of oxygen and generates a lot of carbon dioxide. This lowers tissue pH causing more oxygen to be released from the haemoglobin to where it is required.

6. Myoglobin preferentially picks up oxygen from Hb and is able to act as an oxygen store in the muscle.

7. **Haemoglobin**, which picks up H⁺ generated by the

dissociation of carbonic acid to form haemoglobinic acid (HHb). **Bicarbonate** alone (from this dissociation), and combined with Na⁺ (from the dissociation of NaCl).

206. Plant Systems (page 279)

1. (a) The root system anchors the plant in the soil, and absorbs and transports water and minerals (essential raw materials). It also produces hormones (regulation), stores food, and produces new tissue (growth).
   (b) The shoot system provides support above ground, manufactures food by photosynthesis, enables gas exchange, and transports food and water around the plant.

2. Blue (root and shoot systems): transport, storage, growth
   Red (shoot system): photosynthesis, sexual reproduction
   Black (root system): absorption, anchorage

207. Vascular Tissue in Plants (page 280)

1. Water

2. a) Xylem: Carries water and minerals. Mechanism: **Osmosis** (passive movement of water across a partially permeable membrane from higher to lower concentration of water molecules). Also **tension-cohesion** and (to a lesser extent) root pressure.
   (b) Phloem: Carries sugars and minerals. Mechanism: **Active transport** to load the sugar into the phloem tissue, **osmosis** (water follows sugar into the phloem), **pressure-flow** of the sap along the phloem.

3. A plant must regulate when stomata are open in order to regulate the amount of water lost by transpiration. Losing too much water will cause the plant to wilt.

208. Xylem (page 281)

1. (a) Xylem conducts water and dissolved minerals around the plant (from roots to leaves).
   (b) Xylem forms a continuous tube for the passive process of water transport. Because the transport is passive the cell does not need to be alive.

2. (a) Vessel elements: Provide rapid, low resistance conduction of water.
   (b) Tracheids: Role in water conduction but there is more impedance to water flow than in vessels.
   (c) Fibres (and sclereids): Provide mechanical support to the xylem.
   (d) Xylem parenchyma: Involved in storage.

3. Vascular bundle showing xylem. Other regions are shown in plan view only.

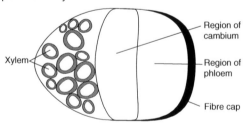

209. Phloem (page 282)

1. Phloem conducts dissolved sugar around the plant from its place of production to where it is required.

2. The phloem needs transport proteins to actively move dissolved nutrients such as sucrose into the phloem stream, The cells must therefore be alive with active plasma membranes to achieve this. Movement of minerals into the xylem in passive and requires no transport proteins.

3. The companion cell keeps the sieve tube cell alive and controls its activity. They are responsible for loading and unloading sugar into the sieve cells.

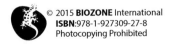

210. Identifying Xylem and Phloem (page 283)

1.

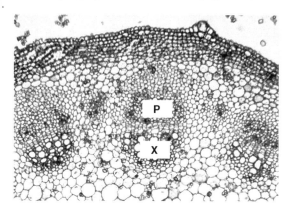

2.

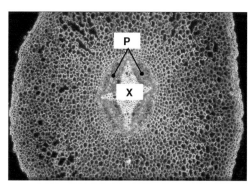

3. A: Fibre cap   D: Cortex
    B: Phloem   E: Vascular cambium
    C: Xylem   F: Pith

211. Uptake at the Root (page 284)

1. (a) Passive absorption of minerals along with the water and
        active transport.
    (b) Apoplastic pathway (about 90%); water moves through the
        xylem and the spaces within cell walls.
        Symplastic pathway; water moves through the cell
        cytoplasm from cell to cell via plasmodesmata.

2. Large water uptake allows plants to take up sufficient
    quantities of minerals from the soil. These are often in very
    low concentration in the soil and low water uptakes would not
    provide adequate quantities.

3. (a) The Casparian strip represents a waterproof barrier to
        water flow through the apoplastic pathway into the stele.
        It forces the water to move into the cells (i.e. move via the
        symplastic route).
    (b) This feature enables the plant to regulate ion uptake, i.e.
        absorb ions selectively. The movement of ions through the
        apoplast cannot be regulated because the flow does not
        occur across any partially permeable membranes

212. Transpiration (page 285)

1. (a) The evaporative loss of water from the leaves and stem of
        a plant.
    (b) Any one of:
    – Transpiration stream enables plants to absorb sufficient
      quantities of the minerals they need (the minerals
      are absorbed with the water and are often in low
      concentration in the soil).
    – Transpiration helps cool the plant.

2. Plants must have their stomata open to exchange gases
    with the environment and when the stomata are open they
    inevitably lose water.

3. Water loss is regulated by the opening and closing of stomata.

4. (a) The plant would lose water from the cells and wilt.
    (b) During a prolonged period without water (e.g. a drought).

5. Water moves by osmosis in all cases. In any order:
    (a) Transpiration pull: Photosynthesis and evaporative
        loss of water from leaf surfaces create higher solute
        concentrations (lower water concentration) in the leaf cells
        than elsewhere, facilitating movement of water down its
        concentration gradient towards the site of evaporation
        (stomata).
    (b) Cohesion-tension: Water molecules cling together and
        adhere to the xylem, creating an unbroken water column
        through the plant. The upward pull on the water creates a
        tension that facilitates movement of water up the plant.
    (c) Root pressure provides a weak push effect for upward
        water movement.

6. Water is moved up the tree by a combination of cohesion-
    tension, transpiration pull, and root pressure, Together these
    process can move water up to heights of far more than 40 m.

213. Investigating Plant Transpiration (page 287)

1. (a) Plot of data below.

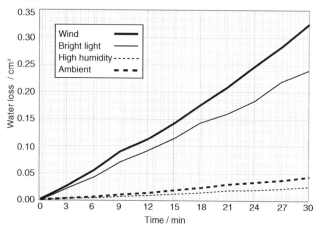

    (b) Independent variable: Time. Explanatory note:
        Environmental conditions are manipulated in that there
        are different treatments, but each condition constitutes a
        controlled variable (or treatment).

2. (a) Transpiration rate in ambient conditions.
    (b) An experimental control enables a measure of the
        biological response in the absence of any of the
        manipulated variables being tested (no treatment). This
        serves as a reference point.
    (c) Wind and bright light increased water loss above the
        ambient (control) conditions.
    (d) Wind and bright light increase transpiration rate by
        increasing evaporative loss from the leaves. High humidity
        reduces transpiration rate by reducing the gradient for
        movement of water from leaf to air.
    (e) In humid conditions, there is a reduced gradient in free
        water concentration between leaf and air, so the rate of
        diffusion of water vapour from the leaf to the environment
        will be slower.

214. Translocation (page 289)

1. (a) The increase in dissolved sugar in the sieve tube cell
        decreases its free water concentration. Water then moves
        into the sieve tube cells by osmosis, creating a pressure
        that pushes the sugar solution through the phloem.
    (b) This means the sugar flows from its site of production
        (leaves) to its site of unloading (roots).

2. Food is manufactured in one region of the plant (the leaves)
    but is required in other regions (e.g. the roots and fruits). It
    must be transported there.

3. (a) Translocation: The transport (around the plant) of the
        organic products of photosynthesis.
    (b) The bulk movement of phloem sap along a gradient in
        hydrostatic pressure (generated osmotically).
    (c) The coupling of sucrose transport (into the transfer cell)
        to the diffusion of H^+ down a concentration gradient

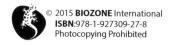
© 2015 **BIOZONE** International
ISBN:978-1-927309-27-8
Photocopying Prohibited

Notes

(generated by a proton pump).

4. Sucrose is transported into the phloem by a protein symport. Sucrose is coupled to the diffusion of hydrogen ions into the cell.

5. The companion cell uses active transport mechanisms (coupled transport of sucrose) to accumulate sucrose to levels 2-3 times those in the mesophyll. The sucrose then moves into the sieve tube cell.

6   (a) The flow of phloem indicates the phloem stream is under pressure.
    (b) The greatest flow rate would be nearest the source (leaves) as this would have the greatest concentration of sugars.
    (c) The stylets penetrate the phloem precisely and without damage. Aphids feeding on different parts of the plant can be used to measure flow rates.

---

215. Experimental Evidence for Plant Transport
(page 291)

1. The ringing experiment shows the phloem is under pressure. It also shows the phloem carries nutrients as growth above the ring is not impeded.

2. It shows that sugars are transported from the leaves to other parts of the plant, but not other leaves.

3. The mass flow hypothesis assumes all fluid in the phloem is moving in the same direction. If some solutes are moving in opposite directions a new hypothesis would be needed to account for this.

4. If sap moved by pressure-flow, then there should be selective pressure for the sieve plate to be lost or become less of a barrier, yet this has not happened. Of course, there are also selective pressures that operate against loss of the sieve plate, such as the need to have discrete yet freely communicating cells.

---

216. Chapter Review (page 292)
No model answer. Summary is the student's own.

---

218. KEY TERMS: Did You Get it? (page 294)

1. (a) Artery
    (b) Vein
    (c) Capillary

2. (a) Systole
    (b) Diastole

3. (a) An ECG or electrocardiogram

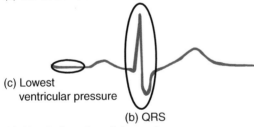

    (c) Lowest ventricular pressure
    (b) QRS
    (d) Ventricular volume is increasing

4. (a) Transpiration (or evapotranspiration)
    (b) Xylem
    (c) Dead
    (d) No

5. (a) Sieve tube end plate
    (b) Phloem
    (c) Alive
    (d) Translocation or transport of sugars
    (e) Sugar or sucrose in solution

6. alveoli (L), ventilation (M), countercurrent exchange (I), gas exchange (E), gills (F), haemoglobin (K), lungs (J), oxyhaemoglobin dissociation curve (A),respiratory gas (G), respiratory pigment (B), spiracles (C), stomata (D), tracheal system (H)

© 2015 **BIOZONE** International
ISBN:978-1-927309-27-8
Photocopying Prohibited